Commodity Fundamentals

Founded in 1807, John Wiley & Sons is the oldest independent publishing company in the United States. With offices in North America, Europe, Australia, and Asia, Wiley is globally committed to developing and marketing print and electronic products and services for our customers' professional and personal knowledge and understanding.

The Wiley Trading series features books by traders who have survived the market's ever-changing temperament and have prospered—some by reinventing systems, others by getting back to basics. Whether a novice trader, professional, or somewhere in-between, these books will provide the advice and strategies needed to prosper today and well into the future.

For a list of available titles, visit our Web site at www.WileyFinance.com.

Commodity Fundamentals

How to Trade the Precious Metals, Energy, Grain, and Tropical Commodity Markets

RONALD C. SPURGA

WILEY

John Wiley & Sons, Inc.

Published by John Wiley & Sons, Inc., Hoboken, New Jersey.
Published simultaneously in Canada.

For general information on our other products and services or for technical support, please contact our Customer Care Department within the United States at (800) 762-2974, outside the United States at (317) 572-3993 or fax (317) 572-4002.

Wiley also publishes its books in a variety of electronic formats. Some content that appears in print may not be available in electronic books. For more information about Wiley products, visit our web site at www.wiley.com.

Library of Congress Cataloging-in-Publication Data:

Spurga, Ronald C.
    Commodity fundamentals : how to trade the precious metals, energy, grain, and tropical commodity markets / Ronald C. Spurga.
       p. cm. — (Wiley trading series)
    Includes index.
    ISBN-13 978-0-471-78851-5 (cloth)
    ISBN-10 0-471-78851-1 (cloth)
    1. Commodity futures.   2. Commodity exchanges.   I. Title.   II. Series.
    HG6046.S658 2006
    332.63'28–dc22

                                              2006009965

Printed in the United States of America.

10   9   8   7   6   5   4   3   2   1

This book is dedicated to the men, women, and children whose lives were irrevocably changed by Hurricane Katrina.

"After so long grief, such nativity!"
        The Comedy of Errors

Acknowledgments

I extend my appreciation to the public information professionals of the New York Mercantile Exchange, the New York Board of Trade, and the Chicago Mercantile Exchange, who took time out from their very busy schedules to graciously provide me with the technical information and contract history and specification clearances so necessary for the production of this book. I also thank Laura Walsh of John Wiley & Sons who shepherded the production process from start to finish and never lost her cool. I also gratefully acknowledge the statistical information presented here on platinum, palladium, and the other precious metals that was provided by Johnson Matthey. Lastly, I would like to give a special of word of thanks to my wife, Marie Colwell, my sun and stars and reason for being.

—Ronald C. Spurga

Contents

PART ONE

Should You Speculate?

CHAPTER 1

Guidelines for Commodity Speculation

During the first day of class, a student of mine said he was confused by the array of financial investments available to him. He knew that a Treasury bill had a minimum investment of $1,000 and would yield him approximately 3 percent, whereas certificates of deposit, bankers acceptances, and commercial paper would yield somewhat more, reflecting their high risk. His question to me was this: "If I can get 3 percent by investing in a government obligation, why should I concern myself with other investments?"

"There's a simple reason—because the inflation rate is 5 percent," I replied.

We then got into a discussion of equities—common stocks—and we both agreed that the autos, airlines, public utilities, farm equipment manufacturers, and domestic steel manufacturers were slumping badly and that this was a reflection of lagging productivity and increased energy costs in our economy in general. If productivity did not increase and oil prices decline, equities would continue to be unattractive.

Were there other investment media? The answer is yes, the commodities markets.

This text is designed to outline the operation of those commodities markets and to provide a sensible approach to investing in them. Organizationally, the text will deal with the mechanics of futures trading in commodities and, building on this base, guide the careful investor to potential investment opportunities.

CHAPTER 2

The Speculator and the Commodity Exchanges

HISTORY AND ORIGIN

When civilization began, trading started. Bartering for different commodities has probably been done since time immemorial. Coined money appeared sometime between 800 BCE and 700 BCE. Soon, instead of bartering as a means of business, coined money was used. Eventually trading had to be done on the basis of future delivery, as a merchant would sell out his complete stock but still have customers waiting to buy. The merchant would then take a partial payment and guarantee delivery at a future date. This type of transaction was probably the beginning of the present-day futures contract.

For nearly 300 years, commodity futures contracts were used. Merchants and processors of food would bid for a farmer's crop before or after planting. Both parties were protected and would not have to fear that drastic price changes of the crop during harvest or delivery would alter the normal course of their business. Today's commodity futures markets still offer this protection.

COMMODITY EXCHANGES

What is a commodity exchange? A commodity exchange is an organized market of buyers and sellers of various types of commodities. It is public to the extent that anyone can trade through member firms. It provides a trading place for commodities, regulates the trading practices of the members, gathers and transmits price information, inspects and governs commodities traded on the exchange, supervises warehouses that store the commodity, and provides means for settling disputes between members. All transactions must be conducted in a "pit" on the exchange floor within certain hours.

FUTURES CONTRACT

What is a futures contract? A futures contract is a contract between two parties in which the buyer agrees to accept delivery of a particular commodity at a specified price from the seller and in a designated month in the future if the commodity is not liquidated before the contract reaches maturity. A futures contract is not an option; nothing in it is conditional. Each contract calls for a specified amount and grade of product. For example, a person buying a February "pork belly" contract at 52.40 in effect is making a legal obligation—in the present—to accept delivery of 38,000 pounds of frozen pork bellies to be delivered during the month of February, for which the buyer will pay 52.40 per pound.

Average traders do not take delivery of a futures contract because they normally close out their position before the futures contract matures. As a matter of fact, a survey conducted by a leading exchange has estimated that less than 3 percent of the contracts traded are settled by actual delivery.

Futures contracts are traded on different exchanges. The major exchanges, the types of contracts in which they trade, and commodity units (shown in parentheses) include:

1. *Chicago Board of Trade (CBOT)*. Wheat, corn, soybeans, soybean meal, soybean oil, iced broilers, silver (5,000 ounces), plywood, oats, gold, Ginnie Maes, commercial paper, Treasury bonds, and Treasury notes.

2. *Chicago Mercantile Exchange*. Live cattle, fresh eggs, live hogs, lumber, russet potatoes, pork bellies, turkeys, stud lumber, feeder cattle, and iced broilers.

3. *International Monetary Market*. A division of the Chicago Mercantile Exchange that trades currency and interest rate futures.

4. *New York Mercantile Exchange (NYMEX)*. Crude oil, natural gas, heating oil, gasoline, gold, silver, copper, aluminum, platinum, and palladium.

5. *New York Board of Trade (NYBOT)*. Coffee, cocoa, cotton, sugar, and orange juice.
6. *Mid America Commodity Exchange (MIDAM)*. Affiliated with the CBOT, it trades grains (in units of 1,000 bushels), silver (1,000 ounces), silver coins (five bags, $1,000 each), gold (1 kilo), hogs (15,000 pounds), and cattle (20,000 pounds).

THE HEDGER AND THE SPECULATOR

A hedger buys or sells a futures contract in order to reduce the risk of loss through price variation. A short hedger sells a futures contract to protect the possible decline in the actual commodity owned by him. A long hedger purchases a futures contract to protect the possible advance in the value of an actual commodity needed to be purchased in the future.

The speculator is an important factor in the volume of future trading today. He (or she) in effect voluntarily assumes the risk, which the hedger tries to avoid with the expectations of making a profit. He is like an insurance underwriter. The largest number of traders on any commodity exchange is the speculator. In order for the hedger to participate, he must have continuous trading interests and activity in the market. This trading activity stems from the role of the speculator, because he involves himself in buying or selling of futures contracts with the idea of making a profit on the advance or decline of prices. The speculator tries to forecast prices in advance of delivery and is willing to buy or sell on this basis. A speculator involves himself or herself in an inescapable risk.

CAN YOU BE A SPECULATOR?

Now, can you be a speculator? Before considering entering the futures market as a speculator, you should understand several facts about the market and also about yourself. In order to enter into the futures market, you must understand that you are dealing with a margin account. Margins are as low as 5 to 10 percent of the total value of the futures contract, so you are obtaining a greater leverage on your capital.

Fluctuations in price are rapid, volatile, and wide. It is possible to make a very large profit in a short period of time, but it is also possible to take a substantial loss. In fact, surveys taken by the United States Department of Agriculture (USDA) have shown that up to 95 percent of the individuals speculating in commodity markets have lost money. This does not mean that some of their trades were not profitable; but after a period of time with a given sum of money, they ended up being losers.

Taking you as an individual, let us see whether you have the characteristics to become a commodity trader. Number one and the most important is that you do not take money that you have set aside for your future or money you need daily to support your family or yourself. Number two, and almost equally important, is that you must be willing to assume losses and be willing to assume these losses with such a temperament that it is not going to affect your everyday life. Money used in the futures market should be money that has been set aside for strictly risk purposes; and if this money is not risk capital, your methods of trading could be seriously affected because you cannot afford to be a loser.

Another very important factor is that you must not feel that you are going to take $1,000, $2,000, $5,000, or $10,000 and place this with a brokerage firm and not follow the daily happenings of the market. Price fluctuations are fast and, as stated before, wide; so you must not only be in contact with your account executive daily but also know and study the technical facts that may be affecting the particular market in which you are speculating.

The individual who makes his first trade by buying a contract on Monday and selling this contract on the following Wednesday, making $600 on $1,000 investment in a period of two days, suddenly says to himself, "Where has this market been all my life? Why am I working? Why not just concentrate on this market if every two days or so I can make six hundred dollars?" This is a fallacy. The next trade, he will feel confident that because of his first profitable trade the market will always go his way even though he is now showing a loss in his position. He still feels that the market will turn around in his direction. If you become married to a particular commodity futures contract and constantly feel that the losses you are taking at the present time will reverse into profits, you are really fighting the market and in most cases fighting a losing battle. This could lead to disaster. There is a saying that you let your profits ride, but liquidate your losses fast.

If in any way you are uneasy with a position you are holding, it is better to liquidate it. If, prior to the time of buying or selling a contract, you are not sure that this is the right step to take, do not take it. To protect yourself against this hazard, you should decide in advance on every trade exactly how much you intend to lose.

Another important point is not to involve yourself in too many markets. It is difficult to know all the technical facts on and be able to follow numerous markets. In addition, if you are in a winning position, be conservative as to how you add additional contracts or pyramid your position. Being conservative will sometimes cause you to miss certain moves in certain markets, and you may feel this to be wrong; but over a long period of time, this conservatism will be profitable to you.

If at this point you feel that you are ready, both financially and mentally, to trade commodities, the next step is to begin the actual mechanics of trading a futures contract.

OPENING AN ACCOUNT

The first important factor is to decide which brokerage firm affords you the best service. To accomplish this, you should do a little research by checking with the various exchanges about different brokerage firms. One quick way is to search online using your web browser. Simply go to www.askjeeves.com and enter "commodity brokerage firms" as your keywords. You will generate a list of such companies.

You should study brokerage firm advertising, market letters, and other information. These should all be presented in a businesslike manner and have no unwarranted claims such as a guarantee of profit without indicating the possibility of loss.

The brokerage firm must be able to handle orders on all commodity exchanges. Do not pick just any account executive in a firm, but one you feel confident to help you make market decisions. Become acquainted with the account executive through phone or personal conversations. That person's knowledge of the factors entering into the market and understanding of current market trends are important in your final choice.

After making a decision on the brokerage firm and the account executive that would be best for you, make contact and request the firm's literature about different kinds of contracts and also request any additional information about the brokerage organization. The account executive will then send you the necessary signature cards required to open an account—and ask you for a deposit of margin money.

You will trade in regulated commodities, and the margin money will be deposited in a segregated fund at the brokerage firm's bank. A segregated fund means that the money will only be used for margin and not for expenses of the brokerage firm.

Now you decide to enter into your first trade. Your account executive and you decide to enter into a December "live cattle" contract on the Chicago Mercantile Exchange. Your order will be executed as follows: Your account executive will place this order with the order desk, who will then transmit the order to the floor of the Chicago Mercantile Exchange. There your order will be executed on the trading floor—in the pit. All technical details connected with the transaction will be handled by the brokerage firm.

Upon filling of your order, the filled order will be transmitted back to your account executive, who then informs you that you have purchased one December live cattle contract at a given price. You will also receive a written confirmation on this transaction. You will now show an open position in December live cattle on the books of the brokerage firm.

CHAPTER 3

The Mechanics of Trading

INTRODUCTION

Let us go back one step to explain in detail how your December cattle buy order was handled on the exchange floor. All buying and selling in the pit are done by open outcry; and every price change is reported on the exchange ticker system. Each firm has brokers in the different pits—that is trading areas for the purpose of buying and selling contracts.

When your order was received on the exchange floor, it was time-stamped and then given to a runner. This is a person who takes the order from the desk on the exchange floor and gives it to one of the brokers in the December cattle trading pit. This broker is then responsible to the brokerage firm to fill that order, if possible, at the stated price. After filling the order, he then has the runner return it to the desk, where it is time-stamped and transmitted back to the order desk at the brokerage house; and the filled order is reported to you.

MARGIN REQUIREMENTS

Futures trading requires you, the trader, to place margin with your brokerage firm. Initial margin is required, and this amount varies with each commodity. The minimum margin is established by each commodity exchange. Additional funds are needed when the equity of your account falls below this level. This is known as a *maintenance margin call*.

All margin calls must be met immediately. Normally you will be given a reasonable amount of time to comply with this request. If you do not comply, the firm has the right to liquidate your trades or a sufficient number of trades to restore your account to margin requirements.

The brokerage firm has the right to raise margin requirements to the customer at any time. This is normally done if the price of the commodity is changing sharply or if it is the brokerage firm's opinion that due to the volatility of the market the margin requirement is not sufficient at that particular time.

Most commodity contracts have a minimum fluctuation and also a maximum fluctuation for any one particular day. For example, if you are trading pork bellies on the Chicago Mercantile Exchange (CME), the fluctuation is considered in points. A point equals $3.80. This means that if you buy a contract at 52.40 and the next price tick is 52.45, you have made a paper profit of 5 points, or $19. The maximum fluctuation on a belly contract is 200 points, so your profit or loss cannot exceed in one day more than 200 points from the previous day's settlement. There are exceptions in some commodity contracts, where the spot month has no limit.

Let us assume that you had originally placed in the hands of your brokerage firm $2,000 margin money and that you and your account executive decide to purchase a December live cattle contract whose initial margin is $1,200 with maintenance of $900. After the purchase of the contract, your account would show initial margin required $1,299, with excess funds of $800. At the end of each day the settlement price of December cattle would be applied to your purchase price, and your account would be adjusted to either an increase due to profit or a decrease due to loss in your contract.

Further, assume that in a period of two or three days, there is a decline in the price of the December cattle contract and your account now shows a loss of $300. Since maintenance margin is only $900 on this contract, you will show an excess of $800 over and above maintenance margin. But in the next four days, suppose there is an additional loss of $900. Your account will now need $100 to maintain the maintenance margin and $400 additional in order to bring your account up to initial margin. Your account executive or someone from the margin department of the brokerage firm will then contact you, stating that you must place additional money with the firm in order to maintain the December cattle contract.

At this point, you must decide whether you should continue with the contract, feeling that it may be profitable in the next few days, and send the brokerage firm the required $400 to maintain your position or assume your loss and sell the contract.

Let us assume that you decide to sell your December contract at this point and that the selling price causes a loss of $400. Added to this loss would be the commission of $40, so your total loss on the transaction would be $440. A confirmation and purchase and sales statement will be sent to you, showing the original price paid for the contract, the price for which it was sold, the gross loss of $400 plus the commission of $40, making the total loss $440, and your new ledger balance on deposit with the firm as $1,560.

As shown in our example, commission was charged only when the contract was closed out. A single commission is charged for each round turn transaction consisting of the creation and liquidation of a single contract.

CONTROLLED DISCRETIONARY AND MANAGED ACCOUNTS

There are two methods of trading your account. The first is the professional approach, in which you and your account executive decide on each trade with no discretion being given directly to your account executive. This method is called a *controlled discretionary or managed account.* Under this method, you are giving your account executive authorization to trade your account at his discretion at any time and as many times as he considers that a trade should be made. The Chicago Mercantile Exchange and the Chicago Board of Trade (CBOT) have rules governing this type of relationship. The following is an excerpt from the CME rule regarding controlled discretionary and managed accounts:

> *No clearing member shall accept or carry an account over which any individual or organization, other than the person in whose name the account is carried, exercises trading authority or control, hereinafter referred to as controlled accounts, unless: "The account is initiated with a minimum of $5,000, and maintained at a minimum equity of $3,750,* regardless of lesser applicable margin requirements. In determining equity the accounts or ledger balances and positions in all commodities traded at the clearing member shall be included. Whenever at the close of any business day the equity, calculated with all open positions figured to the settling price, in any such account is below the required minimum, the clearing member shall immediately notify the customer in person, by telephone or telegraph and by written confirmation of such notice mailed directly to the customer, not later than the close of the following business day. Such notice*

---

* Minimums can be changed by each exchange, so consult your account executive for the current regulations.

shall advise the customer that unless additional funds are promptly received to restore the customer's controlled account to no less than $5,000, the clearing member shall liquidate all of the customer's open futures positions at the Exchange.

In the event the call for additional equity is not met within a reasonable time, the customer's entire open position shall be liquidated. No period of time in excess of five business days shall be considered reasonable unless such longer period is approved in writing by an officer or partner of the clearing member upon good cause shown.

REVIEWING YOUR CONFIRMATIONS AND STATEMENTS

An important factor in trading is that you must be sure that no errors occur in your account. For every trade made you should receive a confirmation, and for every closeout a profit and loss statement, known as a purchase and sale, showing the financial results of each transaction closed out in your account. In addition, a monthly statement showing your ledger balance, your open position, the net profit or loss in all contracts liquidated since the date of your last previous statement, and the net unrealized profit and loss on all open contracts figured to the market should be sent to you.

You should carefully review these statements. Upon receiving a confirmation of a trade, you should immediately check its accuracy as far as type of commodity, month, trading price, and quantity of contracts. If this does not agree with your original order, it should be immediately reported to the main office of your brokerage firm, by which any differences should be explained and adjustments should be made.

If you do not receive a confirmation on a trade after it was orally reported to you by your account executive, be sure to contact him and the main office so that if an error was made it can be corrected immediately. You should receive written confirmation when you deposit money with your brokerage firm. If within a few days you have not received this confirmation, report it immediately to the main office of your brokerage firm.

Never assume that an order has been filled until you receive an oral confirmation from your broker. A ticker or a board that you may be observing can be running several minutes behind and is not the determining factor as to whether your trade was executed. Until you receive this oral confirmation, never reenter an order to buy or sell against that position.

If you receive a confirmation in the mail showing a trade not belonging to you, immediately notify the main office of your brokerage firm and have them explain why this is on a confirmation with your account number. If it is an error, be sure that it is adjusted immediately and a written confirmation sent to you showing the adjustment of the error. If an error is made and it is profitable to you, do not consider this any differently than if it was not profitable. Regardless of whether there is a profit or loss, all errors should be immediately reported to the brokerage firm.

When you request funds to be mailed from your account, be sure that they are received within a few days from the time of your request. If not, contact the accounting department of the brokerage firm to see what is the cause of the delay.

Never make a check out to an individual. Always make your check out to the brokerage firm.

DAY TRADING

Day trading takes place when a buy and sell are made during the trading hours on one particular day. Day trading is not considered to be a sound practice for the new speculator and inexperienced trader. Day trading is something that should be executed only by a sophisticated trader who is in frequent communication with the floor and, even then, on a limited basis.

ORDERS

To trade effectively in the commodity market, there are several basic types of orders.

Market Orders

The most common order is a market order. A market order is one by which you authorize your account executive to buy or sell at the existing price. This is definitely not a predetermined price, but one executed at a bid or offer at that particular moment.

Example: "Buy 5 Feb Pork Bellies at the market."

Limited or Price Orders and "OB" Designation

This type of order to buy or sell commodities at a fixed or "limited" price and the ordinary "market" order are the most common types of orders.

Example: "Buy 3 Jan Silver 463.10."

This limit order instructs the floor broker to buy three contracts of January silver futures at 463.10. Even with this simple order, however, one presumption is necessary—that the market price prevailing is 463.10 or better (OB) when the order enters the pit. If the price is below 463.10, the broker could challenge on the basis that the client may have meant "Buy 3 Jan Silver 463.10 stop." Therefore, while it is always assumed that a limit order means "or better" if possible, it saves confusion and challenges if the "OB" designation is added to the limit price. This is particularly true on orders near the market or on preopening orders with the limit price based on the previous close because no one knows whether the opening will be higher or lower than the close—that is, "Buy 3 Jan Silver 463.10 OB."

Stop Orders (Orders Having the Effect of Market Orders)

Buy Stop. Buy stop orders must be written at a price higher than the price prevailing at the time of entry. If the prevailing price for December wheat is 456 per bushel, a buy stop order must designate a price above 456.

Example: "Buy 20 Dec Wheat 456½ Day Stop." The effect of this order is that if December wheat touches 456½, the order to buy 20 December wheat becomes a market order. From that point, 456½ on, all previous discussion regarding market orders applies.

Sell Stop. Sell stop orders must be written at a price lower than the price prevailing at the time of entry in the trading pit. If the prevailing price of December wheat is 456 per bushel, a sell stop order must designate a price below 456.

Example: "Sell 20 Dec Wheat 455 Day Stop." If this order enters the trading pit with the price of 456 prevailing, the order to sell 20 December wheat becomes a market order. From that point, 455 on, all previous discussion regarding market orders applies.

Buy stop orders have several specific uses. First, if you are short a December wheat at 456 and wish to limit your loss to ½ cent per bushel, the buy stop order at 456½ would serve this purpose. However, it is important to realize that such "stop loss" orders do not actually limit the loss to exactly ½ cent when "elected" or "touched off" because they become market orders and must be executed at whatever price the market conditions dictate.

Another use is when you are without a position and believe that, because of chart analysis or for other reasons, a buy of December wheat at 456½ would signal the beginning of an important uptrend in wheat prices. Thus, the same order to "Buy 20 Dec Wheat 456½ Day Stop" would serve this purpose.

Sell stop orders have the same uses in reverse; that is, if you are long 20 December wheat at 456 and wish to limit this loss to 1 cent per bushel, the sell stop order at 455 would serve this purpose, within the limitations of the market order possibilities. Similarly, if you are without a position and believe that a sale of December wheat at 455 would signal a downtrend in wheat prices and if you wish to be short the market, you could use the order to "Sell 20 Dec Wheat 455 Day Stop" for this purpose.

Stop-Limit Orders (Variations of Stop Orders)

Stop-limit orders should be used by you when you wish to give the floor broker a limit beyond which he cannot go in executing the order that results when a stop price is "elected."

This instructs the broker that when the price of 456½ is reached and "elects" this stop order, instead of making it a market order, it becomes a limited order to be executed at 456½ (or lower), but no higher than 456½.

Example: "Buy one Feb Pork Belly 58.10 Day Stop Limit 58.25" (or any other price above 58.10). This instructs the broker that when the price of 58.10 "elects" the stop order, instead of making it a market order, it becomes a limited order to buy at 58.25 (or lower), but no higher, as with any limit order.

Stop-limit orders are particularly useful to you when you have no position and wish to enter a market via the stop order but want to put some reasonable limit as to what you will pay. On the other hand, stop-limit orders are not useful to you when you have an open position and wish to prevent a loss beyond a certain point. The reason is that by limiting the broker to a certain price after a "stop-loss order" is elected, *you also run the risk that the market may exceed the limit too fast for the broker to execute.* This would leave you with your original position because the broker would have to wait for the return to the limit before executing. With a straight stop (no limit) order, the broker executes "at the market."

Example: "Buy 1 Feb Pork Belly 58.10 Day Stop Limit 58.25." Suppose the market moves to 58.10, but only 20 February pork bellies are offered at that price. Your broker in the pit catches the seller's eye first and buys 20, and your broker misses the sale. Your broker then bids 58.20, but the best offer is 58.30. He bids 58.25, but the offer at 58.30 remains unchanged. Then another broker bids for and buys February pork bellies at 58.30, and the market moves on up. Your broker is left with no execution to your order unless the market later declines to your limit making a fill possible.

If you did not have a position, you might be disappointed, but you would be unhurt financially. However, if you had a position and were trying to limit your loss, you would have defeated your purpose with the stop-limit order if you truly wanted "but" after the stop was elected.

Stop-limit orders on the sell side have exactly the same uses, advantages, and disadvantages as discussed previously but in reverse:

Example: "Sell 20 Dec Wheat 455 Day Stop Limit." This means that when the market declines to 455 per bushel, the broker may sell at 455 (or higher), but no lower.

Another example: "Sell 1 Feb Pork Belly 58.25 Stop Limit 58.10." This instructs the broker to sell a belly after the stop price of 58.25 is reached and "elects" the stop order but no lower than 58.10.

MIT (Market-If-Touched) Orders

By adding MIT (market-if-touched) to a limit order, the limit order will have the effect of a market order when the limit price is reached or touched. This type of order is useful to you when you have an open position and if a certain limit price is reached.

Example: "Sell 1 Sept Sugar 950 MIT." The floor broker is told that if and when the price of September sugar rises to 9½ cents per pound, he is to sell one contract at the market. At this price of 9½ cents, all prior discussion on market orders applies.

Under certain market conditions, not enough contracts are bid at 9½ cents to fill all offers to sell. Thus you may see your straight limit price appear on the ticker, but your broker fails to make the sale.

By adding MIT to the limit price, you will receive an execution because the order becomes a market order if the price is touched. However, the price will not necessarily be a good one in your eyes, since it became a market order when touched.

The same reasoning is true on the buy side of MIT orders, but in reverse. Assume you are short one contract of September sugar, with the prevailing price at 9½ cents per pound, and you want to cover or liquidate your short at 9 cents.

Example: "Buy 1 Sept Sugar 9¢ MIT." If and when the price of September sugar declines to 9 cents per pound, the floor broker must buy one contract at the market. Aside from the disadvantages of any market order, the MIT designation on the buy order prevents the disappointment that might arise if a straight limit buy at 9 cents were entered without the MIT added.

Spread Orders

Spread is a simultaneous long and short position in the same or related commodity. Thus a spread order would be to buy one month of a certain commodity and sell another month of the same commodity or to buy one month of one commodity and sell the same or another month of a related commodity.

Example: "Buy 5 July Beans Market and Sell 5 May Beans Market" or "Buy 10 Kansas City Dec Wheat Market and Sell 10 Chicago May Wheat Market."

Another example: "Buy 5 May Corn Market and Sell 5 May Wheat Market."

In the example of the related commodity spread, normally the reason you would use such a spread is that you expect to make a profit out of an expected tightness in the Corn Market, hoping that the corn contract will gain in value faster than the wheat.

There may be a situation where you have a position either long or short in the commodity and want to change to a nearer or more distant option of the same commodity. For example, you are long 5,000 bushels of May soybeans on May 20 and want to avoid a delivery notice by moving your position forward into the July option. The basic spread order would be: "Buy 5 July Beans Market and Sell 5 May Beans Market." Sometimes you may prefer not to use market orders, in which case you use the difference spread.

Example: "Buy 5 July Beans and Sell 5 May Beans July 2¢ Over." Even though the prices of the two options are not specified, the broker is allowed to execute at any time he can do so with July selling at 2 cents or less above May. Over or under designations are a necessity for clarity to the floor broker. Omitting either is like omitting the price.

All orders, except market orders, can be canceled prior to execution. Naturally, a market order is executed immediately upon reaching the pit, so its cancellation is almost impossible.

ADDITIONAL TRADING TECHNIQUES

Two additional trading techniques are the *switch* (also referred to as the spread or straddle) and the *cash and carry*.

Switch (Spread/Straddle)

1. Look at nearby months:

December Gold	**April Gold**
396 Sell 1 contract @	415.80

Assumption: Inflation will continue to make gold a desirable investment.

2. Decide to buy April and sell December.

3. Tell broker to "buy switch" at $19.80 (415.80 – 396). A switch requires 50 percent margin because of offsetting positions.

4. Hold position three to four weeks, look at contract months, and then tell broker to "unwind switch." See the following equation:

December Gold	**April Gold**
Buy 1 contract @ 446	Sell 1 contract @ 475.80
396	415.80
Loss on Dec. + (50)	Gain on April + 60.00

Net Gain = $10/03. × 100.03. = $1,000.

Cash and Carry

The cash-and-carry technique is shown in the following equation:

December Gold	**June Gold**
703	758

Purchase 100 ounces of gold @ $703 in cash market sell 1 contract gold on COMEX to mature in June @ $758.

Premium over Cash Market

$$\frac{55}{703} \times \frac{360}{180} \times \frac{100}{1} = 15\%$$

Borrow the $70,000 at 14% (fixed rate).
Around June deliver 100 ounces to close out the COMEX contract.
Profit = $75,800 – ($70,300 + $4,921 int. cost) = $579

SUMMARY

Here are some rules for successful trading:

1. *Go with the trend.* Go with prices when they leave a congestion. When wheat, beans, corn, and soybean meal make new season highs, the trader should go along regardless of his feelings. The pit prices are the supreme judge of who is right and who is wrong. The markets are not straight, one-way—there are reactions. If you desire, buy half of your commitment on new highs and the other half on the reaction. Just remember: The reaction may not come for some time.

2. *Get out and watch.* If after making a new season high the markets close lower on volume, *get out and watch*, as it indicates a danger sign.

If it closes on the bottom and opens with a down gap the next day, *absolutely get out and wait or go short against the high or gap.* The reverse is true on season lows.

3. *Always trade with stops.* The first loss is the cheapest loss. The place to pray is church, not in the pits. If you are stopped out and the market reverses, go with it again.

4. *Let your profits ride. Move your stops with the market. Never* decide on your profit when the market breaks out of its range. This does not apply when it trades within a range.

5. *Buy the strongest option of the commodity.* If you want to spread, sell the weakest.

6. *Never let a profit turn into a loss.*

7. *Do not overtrade.* You will be whipsawed to death in a turbulent market as prices go back and forth until the proper level is found.

8. *If you don't know, stay out!* The best traders are those who don't trade every tick.

9. *If you are wrong.* If you are wrong, one contract is too many. If you are right, one contract is not enough within your prudent margin requirements.

10. *Be long.* If the market closes on new season highs or new season highs close on the limit up, *be long* that contract. The reverse is true.

11. *Also be long.* If all the other markets close lower on the bottom and one commodity closes higher, be long that contract. The reverse is true.

12. *Be short.* If one contract closes limit up and finally at the end of the day, one of the other contracts comes limit up, be short the contract that closes limit up last.

13. *Have self-control.* Do not go overboard.

14. *Be even on the eve of a government report.* Then go with the market.

15. *Be respectful of gaps.* Most are closed; but the unclosed few are strong trend indicators.

PART TWO

Techniques for Trading Physical Commodities

CHAPTER 4

Technical Analysis

T echnical analysis deals exclusively with market activity to develop a price forecast. As an investor, you are looking for a way to make a prediction about the future price of a commodity. Technical analysts look at prices, trading volume, and open interest to determine price forecasts.

The oldest method of technical market analysis has to do with interpreting the patterns of investment on price charts. The two most common charts are "bar" and "point and figure." Bar charts illustrate the range and close of prices during a fixed time period (weekly). Point and figure charts use a figured amount of price change to illustrate forward and backward pattern investments.

A typical bar chart is shown in Figure 4.1. This chart shows a clear downtrend in the June 1982 gold contract traded on the Commodity Exchange Index (COMEX) in New York. Gold trading has enjoyed tremendous growth since it began in the United States in 1975. From January to December of 1981, 10.3 million contracts have traded on the COMEX. This compares to 8 million for all of 1980, 6.5 million for 1979, 3.7 million for 1978, 1 million in 1977, and 0.5 million in 1976. The bull market in gold began in the early 1970s with prices at about $25 per ounce. As world inflation accelerated, gold moved to $200 per ounce by December 1974. At this point, gold became available to Americans; but instead of the instant bull market many people anticipated, prices fell to $100 by mid-1976. Then the real move began. Gold reached $875 in early 1980 but collapsed soon after. By the end of March 1980, the nearest gold future fell to $450, another

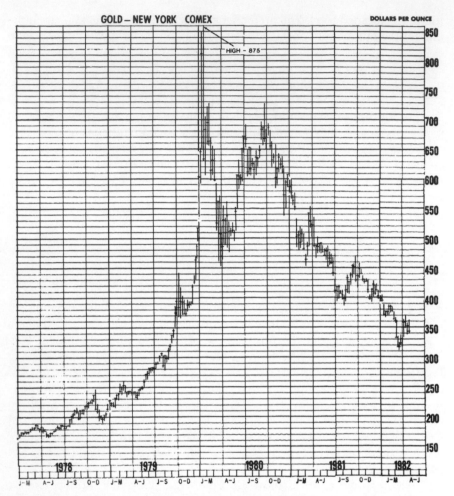

GOLD – NEW YORK COMEX   DOLLARS PER OUNCE

HIGH – 875

Figure 4.1   Gold—Commodity Exchange Index (COMEX)

50 percent decline. This one occurred in less than three months. Then we saw a rally above $700 for the nearby contract, and the present decline began. The bear move coincided with falling prices of other commodities and with a general decline in inflation rates. The $400 level has twice provided good support for gold. However, any penetration of the $400 support level would signal new lows for the contract. Gold settled at $566.50 per ounce in June 2006 as hedge funds liquidated positions. More than 30 million ounces of gold are now traded annually on COMEX.

You should also remember that "open interest" refers to the number of open contracts. It also refers to unliquidated purchases or sales and never to their combined total. You are concerned with open interest because the greater the number of contracts outstanding, the easier it will be for you to liquidate a position without seriously depressing the price of the contract. High volume and open interest levels suggest that increasing volatility will be experienced in the markets. This calls for even greater diversification and proper money management techniques on the part of the investor.

For a further discussion of technical analysis, see Robert D. Edwards and John Magee, *Technical Analysis of Stock Trends* (Springfield, MA: John Magee Inc., 1948); Perry Kaufman, *Commodity Trading Systems and Methods* (New York: John Wiley & Sons, 1979); and Jerome C. Cohen, et al., *Investment Analysis and Portfolio Management*, 5th ed. (Homewood, IL: Irwin, 1987).

CHAPTER 5

The Risks of Speculation

I t is not the intention of this book to convince you to speculate in commodities. My feeling is that the would-be investor should be continually reminded that commodities are fraught with risk.

To reinforce this point, consider what happens after you have decided you do want to speculate and you have selected a broker. The first order of business your broker undertakes is to have you sign a *risk disclosure statement*. This statement is furnished to you because Rule 1.55 of the Commodity Futures Trading Commission (CFTC) requires it. (You can obtain a complete list of certified contacts at www.cftc.gov.)

The risk of loss in trading commodity futures contracts can be substantial. You should therefore carefully consider whether such trading is suitable for you in light of your financial condition. In considering whether to trade, you should be aware of the following:

1. You may sustain a total loss of the initial margin funds and any additional funds that you deposit with your broker to establish or maintain a position in the commodity futures market. If the market moves against your position, you may be called upon by your broker to deposit a substantial amount of additional margin funds, on short notice, in order to maintain your position. If you do not provide the required funds within the prescribed time, your position may be liquidated at a loss, and you will be liable for any resulting deficit in your account.

2. Under certain market conditions, you may find it difficult or impossible to liquidate a position. This can occur, for example, when the market makes a "limit move."

3. Placing contingent orders, such as stop-loss or stop-limit orders, will not necessarily limit your losses to the intended amounts because market conditions may make it impossible to execute such orders.

4. A spread position may not be less risky than a simple long or short position.

5. The high degree of leverage that is often obtainable in futures trading because of the small margin requirements can work against you as well as for you. The use of leverage can lead to large losses as well as gains.

This brief statement cannot, of course, disclose all the risks and other significant aspects of the commodity markets. You should therefore carefully study futures trading before you trade.

You are reminded of the following:

1. Losses can be quite substantial.

2. You can very well lose all original and variation margin. If you run out of margin money, the brokerage could sell your house to satisfy any additional indebtedness.

3. Stop-loss or limit orders don't necessarily get you out of a losing position.

4. You can lose as much on a spread as on an "outright," even though the margin is 50 percent less for a spread.

5. Leverage is a two-way street. It is only attractive if you are on the right side of the market.

If this has not frightened you off, let us push ahead with some tales of gold.

PART THREE

Speculating in Metals

CHAPTER 6

Gold

OVERVIEW

Gold, a dense metallic element, is unaltered by air, heat, moisture, and most solvents. The near indestructibility of gold means that the vast majority of all this metal ever mined is still in existence. Some is held in jewelry, coins, and medals; some is in industrial use and equipment; some is hoarded; and some is in government hands. Hoarding of gold is common in many countries thanks to the centuries-old use of gold as the ultimate standard of value in times of depression, inflation, or unrest.

People began using gold as a standard of value in the second millennium BCE when gold and silver became the currency of Mediterranean trade. Gold and silver coins continued to be principal forms of money for approximately 3,500 years.

In the 17th and 18th centuries, there was a move away from gold coins in favor of paper currencies as people deposited their gold with local goldsmiths for safekeeping and received receipts for the amount deposited. These receipts then circulated as money in place of gold itself. As the industrial society developed, increasing demand for money stocks in order to carry on expanded commerce, paper came to replace gold for normal, everyday transactions. Paper was easier to carry than gold; and as long as people accepted paper in lieu of gold, it served as a convenient means of payment.

Great Britain was the first country in modern time to officially tie its paper currency to gold when, in 1816, it stated the value of an ounce of gold in terms of a fixed amount of British currency. Other European countries followed suit, and eventually so did the United States. The United States first linked the value of the dollar to a fixed amount of gold in 1900.

Under the original "full" gold standard, the amount of a nation's currency in circulation was closely tied to the amount of gold in the country's reserves. Currency and gold coins moved freely from country to country as nations settled their international trading accounts.

Later, a gold-bullion standard existed briefly under which nations redeemed their bank notes with gold bullion rather than with coin. Problems arose with this system, however, and the international community switched to a modified gold exchange standard whereby settlement of international accounts was made in major paper currencies, chiefly the U.S. dollar and the British pound.

Although gold, at least theoretically, remained the underlying base for the gold exchange standard throughout much of the 20th century, a number of changes in the international monetary system reduced the importance of gold in practice.

Under the Bretton Woods Agreement of 1944, the central banks of the world set up a formal system to keep the U.S. dollar exchange rates for their currencies within a 1 percent range above or below a declared par value. In addition, the signatory banks agreed that the U.S. dollar would be the kingpin of the international money system. Moreover, they determined that an ounce of gold would have a fixed value of $35.

This system collapsed in 1971 when the United States, after suffering substantial and continuing gold losses, refused to continue converting foreign-held dollars into gold and later twice devalued the dollar. This led to today's widespread floating of major currencies. A two-tier gold market was established in 1968: a private or free market and an "official" rate at which the price of gold was pegged for making international payments among countries' central banks. The extensive floating of currencies, however, further diminished the role of the precious metal in the conduct of such transactions.

Beginning in June 1976, the International Monetary Fund (IMF), which was established in 1947 as an agency of the United Nations to foster international monetary cooperation, held monthly auctions of gold. The "profit" from these auctions was the difference between the IMF's selling price and the "official" IMF price of $41 an ounce. This profit, about $96 an ounce, had put about $1 billion into the trust fund for 61 of the world's less-developed nations by the end of 1977. These nations borrowed from the fund on easy terms.

Leading members of the IMF reached an agreement in Jamaica in January 1976 under which central banks, starting early in 1978, would be free to buy and sell bullion without restriction at the free-market price; and an

IMF amendment put an end to the "official" price of gold. Together, these two actions together effectively and finally demonetized gold.

Starting in the late 1970s, the price of gold began an historic rise, soaring to over $850 an ounce in early 1980. The price fell steadily throughout much of the 1980s and 1990s and bottomed at around $260 in 2001. Since then the price has been rising; and as this book was written, it was over $500 an ounce. Many market forecasters believe the long term trend for gold continues to be bullish, and they anticipate significantly higher prices in the next several years.

London, with its long-standing ties to South Africa, has always been an important center for dealings in gold. Today, London prices are still watched as price guidelines for the free market in gold.

Five international bullion houses make up the London Gold Market. Representatives of these five firms meet twice daily, at 10:30 A.M. and 3:00 P.M. London time, for the purpose of establishing a morning and an afternoon daily price fixing. Bids and offers are brought to the meetings from banking and industrial clients of the five houses. When buy and sell orders can be consummated at a price satisfactory to all, the fixed price has been established. London Gold Market prices serve as a benchmark for private gold dealing throughout the world.

Another world gold-trading center is Zurich. Switzerland has long been a gold-conscious country, and in recent years Zurich has emerged as a major world gold-trading center. During the 1968 world monetary crisis, prior to the establishment of the two-tier system, the London Market was forced to suspend business for a two-week period. The Swiss were quick to take advantage of the vacuum thus created and seized the opportunity to expand their business. Ranking close to London in importance, Zurich continues to be a major center for gold dealings.

DEMAND

Prices and price fluctuations of gold on the free world market are not the result of chance but are determined by powerful economic and psychological forces that continuously change. In order to predict price trends effectively, these forces must be analyzed and evaluated continually. As is true with any other commodity, the primary factors influencing gold prices are supply and demand. Supplies are obtained from production of new gold or from private or official stockpiles. The aggregate consumption of gold reflects demand.

There are two categories of demand for gold: (1) bullion used for hoarding and investment and (2) fabricated products taking a wide variety of forms. While there are gray areas for the latter, such as jewelry, which is sometimes bought more for investment than decoration, gold is a critical element in many industrial processes, primarily in the field of electronics. Computers, for example, depend on gold circuitry, while gold's imperviousness to corrosion ensures reliable performance of electronics and telecommunications equipment.

Gold is also used in medicine, in dentistry, and in reflective glass. Biochemists use gold to bond with compound materials in the creation of drugs, and genetic researchers use gold to examine the genetic materials of cells.

Fabrication demand for gold is estimated to have been 82.6 million ounces in 2005, which was up from 80.9 million ounces in 2004 and was the highest level since 91.2 million ounces were used in 2001. It was off 21 percent from the peak annual gold use of 104.6 million ounces in 1998. In general, gold fabrication demand falls when prices rise, mostly because higher prices adversely affect demand for gold jewelry. It should be noted again that gold jewelry is thought of as an investment in parts of the world, particularly in Asia and the Middle East. Thus, in these regions, gold jewelry demand is not particularly price sensitive and can even rise in line with price increases.

By far, jewelry is the largest single source of physical gold demand, accounting for about 70 percent of fabrication demand, followed by about 23 percent for industrial uses and about 7 percent for dental uses.

Numerous factors undoubtedly influence total gold demand. Substitutions of other metals, if less expensive, will be attempted in some areas if consumer resistance to higher gold prices is widespread. War or the threat of war always increases gold demand as well.

But these factors aside, gold demand should fundamentally reflect a country's monetary situation. For example, wide fluctuations in foreign exchange rates and unstable financial institutions drive gold demand by stirring distrust of paper currencies. Uncontrolled inflation, fed by higher oil prices or a growing balance of payment deficits, would likewise spur demand for gold, whose intrinsic value is less susceptible than paper money to inflationary erosion. Conversely, improvements in the monetary situation would likely weaken demand for gold.

The potential impact that gold investing, speculating, and hoarding can have on demand necessitates that methods for measuring demand for gold be general rather than precise. One approach emphasizes gold's countercyclical tendency. Advocates of this approach compare trends in gold and, in particular, the stock market in order to emphasize inverse relations between the two. The rationale for this approach is that gold is the ultimate hedge. Consequently, demand for gold should be highest in periods of recession, depression, or growing inflation and lower in periods of relative prosperity.

Another approach to measuring gold demand is to treat general commodity-price trends as indicators of gold-demand trends. The anticipation is that a significant upturn in commodity markets will stimulate fears of inflation and increase demand for gold.

In general, historical trends confirm that demand for gold is indeed influenced by monetary and emotional considerations, with fear of inflation being the greatest motivator. In the period 1979-1980, for example, high inflation, rising crude oil prices, and a deteriorating situation in the Middle East forced gold prices to $850 per troy ounce. By contrast, gold prices during the relatively stable, low-inflation five-year period ending 2001 ranged from $271 to $331 per troy ounce.

More recently, in 2004, gold showed a strong negative daily correlation of –0.92 to the dollar index. "When the dollar falls in value relative to other currencies and real assets," notes the *CRB Commodity Yearbook 2005*, "the price of gold rises when quoted in terms of the weaker dollar." Also fueling higher gold prices in 2004 was the relative strength of the United States and global economies, which increased industrial and jewelry demand for gold.

SUPPLY

The *CRB Commodity Yearbook 2005* reports that world mine production of gold was 2.590 million kilograms in 2004, slightly less than the record 2.600 million kilograms produced in 2001. The largest producer, South Africa, represented 15 percent of total 2003 production, followed by Australia (11 percent), the United States (11 percent), China (8 percent), Russia (7 percent), and Canada (5 percent). The U.S. share declined 7.0 percent to 277,000 kilograms, its lowest production level since 1989.

World monetary institution and central bank holdings of gold fell to 909.58 million troy ounces in 2004, a level that is equivalent to $364 billion, assuming a gold price of $400 per ounce. This total, which represents a steady decline in the gold held by world monetary institutions and central banks over the past six years, is near a postwar low. This reduction is the result of sales by some institutions to raise cash and reduce storage costs.

Modern gold exploration, unlike the images of panhandlers from the California Gold Rush 150 years ago, is technology driven. Surface ore deposits have long been found, and geologists must now rely on physical and chemical characteristics of rocks to locate new deposits. Geologists drill test prospective sights to test samples from various locations to determine the presence of gold and the quality of any deposits.

If the gold is close to the surface, a mining company can use an open-pit mine, whereas deeply buried deposits require an underground mine. Even an open-pit mine can require a year to build, however, and the time from discovering gold to excavating it can be as much as five years. That's because mines are often located in remote regions and require an expensive infrastructure to support them, including roads, towns, storage areas, and administrative offices. Often a number of government authorities must sign off on any finalized plans for mining in a given regions as well, and the mining company must set up a reclamation process to restore the land once mining activities cease.

Equally important, a mining company must determine the metallurgical quality of the gold so as to determine how best to process the gold. The first step in processing gold ore is to crush the rock taken from the ground. The crushed rock undergoes various treatments, depending on its mineral content, and then moves on to a processing location.

Cynaide is added to low-grade ore, which dissolves the gold, allowing it to be collected. High-grade ore gets more extensive treatment. First the ore undergoes a grinding process, followed by alternative treatments depending on the mineral makeup of the ore. Oxide, for example, is combined with cyanide to dissolve the gold; whereas refractory ore, which contains carbon, is heated to 1,000 degrees Fahrenheit. This burns off sulphide and carbon, after which the refractory ore is also combined with cyanide.

Next, the gold extracted from the leaching process is deposited on activated carbon, allowing the gold to be chemically stripped. This impure gold is melted into bars that are approximately 90 percent pure gold—bars that are then shipped to a refinery for further processing.

The refining process melts the 90 percent gold bars and combines the gold with chloride. This converts remaining impurities to chlorides that float on top of the gold. The remaining gold is 99 percent gold. It is then cast into electrodes through which an electric current is passed, converting the gold to 99.99 percent pure gold, which is then made into bullion bars.

TRADING

Private investment in gold falls into two major categories: (1) paper transactions, which are largely confined to the futures markets and to gold mine securities, and (2) the physical ownership of gold. The latter entails either holding small bars of gold, as is especially popular in Asia, the Middle East, and the Far East, or the purchase of gold bullion, again for investment or speculative purposes, which is common in European countries.

A futures contract for gold is a legally binding instrument to buy or sell a designated quantity of gold at a specific time period in the future, at a price agreed upon today. The contract details the standards the gold must meet in order to be acceptable for delivery. Price is arrived at through an open, competitive auction system.

To enter into a contract, a buyer or seller is required by the brokerage firm and by the exchange to provide a security deposit, usually called margin, which normally is less than 10 percent of the contract's value. These security deposits control large amounts of money at a relatively small cost. Brokers must execute all purchases and sales of futures contracts, for which they receive a nominal commission fee. The procedure of opening an account and entering an order is simple. It is no more difficult to buy or sell gold futures contracts than to buy or sell securities.

Once a trader has taken a position in the market by buying or selling one or more contracts, he has two options: either (1) maintain the position until the contract matures and then accept or make delivery; or (2) offset the contract before maturity by assuming a position equal and opposite to the original trade. In other words, if a trader originally bought one gold contract, he (or she) could liquidate or offset by selling that contract. If he originally sold a contract, he could offset by buying it back. In both cases his liquidating trade must be made for the same delivery month and on the same exchange as the original contract. Approximately 97 percent of all commitments are offset in this manner, rather than by delivery.

Participants in the gold futures market may be classified into two general groups—hedgers and speculators. Although the trading patterns of these groups may overlap, their motivations for participation in the market are distinctly different.

Hedgers use the market principally as a marketing and price-protection tool for establishing, in the present, the price at which they will buy or sell their inventory of gold at a future date. A hedger, then, is someone involved in the physical production, processing, handling, or marketing of an actual commodity, in this instance gold.

The hedger uses gold futures as a financial management tool. Proper use of the market can assist him in stabilizing income, freeing working capital, reducing procurement costs, reducing inventory costs, ensuring contract obligations, and providing flexibility in timing of purchases and sales. Hedgers in the gold market might include miners, smelters, gold depositories, gold fabricators, and industrial users of fabricated gold.

A speculator does not deal in or handle a physical commodity. His concern is with price changes only. He is motivated by the potential for making a profit from volatility in commodity prices. He uses his risk capital in an attempt to take advantage of favorable price fluctuations in the market by buying futures when he thinks they will go up in price and selling when he believes they will go down in price. His participation in the market provides the liquidity that affords trading opportunities for hedgers at low cost.

Both the hedger and the speculator are essential to each other and to the successful functioning of a liquid futures market. If the futures market provided no economic function for the hedger, there would be less need for it to exist. And without the speculator to assume the hedger's risk, there would be no market. Together, they provide the needed liquidity to facilitate entry into and egress from the futures market.

Speculators, as mentioned, invest in the market hoping to benefit from volatility. Their goal is to correctly anticipate and take advantage of price swings. Common triggers for such price swings include concern about erosion in the value of paper money; rising inflation rates; political crises leading to armed confrontation, especially between superpowers; disruption of Middle East oil supplies to importing nations; and hedge fund buying.

CHAPTER 7

Silver

OVERVIEW

Silver, a white metallic element, conducts heat and electricity better than any other metal. Next to gold, it is the most malleable of all metals. Silver is both an industrial and a precious metal and has been mined since ancient times, when many silver deposits were near the earth's surface. Like gold, silver was used by ancient civilizations as currency, replacing the earlier barter system of commerce.

Silver's extreme malleability makes it too soft for many uses, requiring that a hardening agent—generally copper—be added to the silver. Sterling silver is metal that consists of 92.5 percent silver and 7.5 percent copper. While silver is not very chemically active, it does combine with sulfur and sulfides to form silver sulfide—or tarnish—on its surface.

Silver is most commonly found in combination with other elements and is therefore mined together with zinc, lead, or copper. The biggest U.S. producers of silver are Nevada, Idaho, Alaska, and Arizona. As an industrial metal, silver is used in photography, electronics, and glass and as an antibacterial agent.

Pricing of silver, like that of gold, can be very volatile. In 1979 silver began trading at $6.02 per ounce and ended the year at $28 per ounce. The $28 price is especially remarkable when one considers that the production cost of silver is only $7 per ounce.

The sharp rise in silver prices in 1979 was due in part to a worsening energy crisis and the deterioration of the United States dollar. Other factors were the Indian government's decision to ban the export of silver, as well

41

as a reduction in silver supplied from recycling operations. Commodities folklore is also replete with stories of how in this period Nelson Bunker Hunt, a billionaire Texas oilman, together with Arab investors, purchased 23 million ounces of silver in October 1979. The Hunt group ultimately controlled 60 million ounces of silver by the time the price of silver collapsed in January 1980.

After reaching $28, silver fell to an average price of $8 an ounce by 1981 and $6 an ounce in 1982. In 1982, Peru, Mexico, and Canada tried to institute a marketing organization similar to the Organization of Petroleum Exporting Countries (OPEC) to maintain the price of silver at desired levels. This effort was only modestly successful. Also in 1982 the United States Department of the Interior suspended the sale of silver from its strategic stockpile. These moves helped prevent the price of silver from falling below $4 an ounce.

Throughout much of the 1990s, silver prices stayed in a range of $4 to $6 an ounce. In 2005, the price broke to the upside and soared as high as $9. As is the case with gold, many analysts believe the ingredients are in place for a long-term bull market in silver.

DEMAND

Total fabrication demand for silver in 2004 was 836.7 million ounces, down slightly from 853.4 million ounces in 2003. The biggest driver of demand in 2004 was acceleration in the global gross domestic product, which fueled a 5 percent increase in industrial fabrication to 367.1 million ounces. At this level, fabrication demand was just a fraction less than at its peak in 2000—the height of the technology bubble.

Also driving total fabrication demand was a 15 percent increase–to 41.1 million ounces—in the fabrication of coins and medals. This rise was a result of the minting of commemorative coins in Portugal, Spain, and Canada as well as of the demand for U.S. proof coin sets.

Jewelry and silverware fabrication totals fell in 2004 due largely to increases in local silver prices in India. Meanwhile, jewelry and silver fabrication in East Asia—especially China and Thailand—showed significant gains over 2003 levels.

Photographic demand slipped 6 percent in 2004, but some areas of demand in this sector actually grew. For example, traditional photographic demand in China experienced 6 percent growth overall.

As of 2002, the United States was the largest consumer of silver for industrial purposes (20.2 percent of world consumption), followed by India and Japan (both 14.7 percent) and Italy (6.5 percent). Photographic materials represent the biggest percentage of industrial uses of silver (54.4 percent of total usage), followed by electrical contacts and conductors (15.7 percent), brazing alloys and solders (4.5 percent), catalysts (3.3 percent), batteries (2.8 percent), jewelry (2.6 percent), sterling ware (2.5 percent), silver plate (2.1 percent), and mirrors (1.3 percent). For a historical comparison of world consumption and supplies, see Tables 7.1 and 7.2. As of mid-2006, investment demand for silver was also being met by exchange-traded funds (ETFs), which are essentially mutual funds that trade commodities and trade on exchanges.

TABLE 7.1 World Silver Consumption

	World Silver Consumption (millions of ounces)						
	1979	**1978**	**1977**	**1976**	**1975**	**1974**	**1973**
Industrial Uses:							
United States	166	160	154	170	158	177	196
Japan	65	64	63	61	46	47	69
West Germany	37	26	60	51	39	60	65
Italy	33	42	34	32	29	39	42
France	21	22	21	19	21	16	14
United Kingdom	27	29	32	28	28	25	31
India	19	20	18	18	13	15	13
Other	42	41	36	43	43	32	48
Total—Industrial Uses	410	404	418	422	377	411	478
Coinage:							
United States	.1	.1	.4	1.3	2.7	1.0	.9
Canada	.3	.3	.3	8.4	10.4	8.6	1.4
France	7.7	11.1	6.9	6.7	5.2	3.6	.1
Austria	5.0	9.5	3.0	6.9	13.4	5.6	6.6
West Germany	3.7	3.6	2.6	2.9	4.3	8.8	9.5
Others	6.0	10.4	6.0	3.5	2.8	.1	10.7
Total—Coinage	22.8	35.0	19.2	29.7	38.8	27.7	29.2

TABLE 7.2   World Silver Supplies

| | World Silver Supplies (millions of ounces) 1973–1979 | | | | | | |
	1979	1978	1977	1976	1975	1974	1973
New production	271	265	268	247	242	237	254
U.S. Treasury stocks	—	—	—	1	3	1	1
Scrap recovery	81	87	80	76	73	66	60
Liquidation of (additions to) speculative inventories	30	14	20	(4)	(21)	33	62
Other sources	51	68	69	132	119	100	130
Total available supplies	433	434	437	452	416	437	507

SUPPLY

Silver is the most plentiful of the precious metals. Its yearly world production in 2004 of 879.2 million ounces was slightly less than 2003's total of 883.1 million ounces. Because silver is rarely found isolated in ores, it is primarily mined as a by-product metal with copper, lead, or zinc. The demand and price factors for these metals directly affect the supply and price of raw silver.

An important secondary source of silver is the reclamation of silver and silver-bearing waste solutions, especially from the photographic industry. Other sources include both domestic and foreign holdings by governments and individuals.

Silver production from primary mines increased 9 percent in 2004, for a total of 188.5 million ounces, which represented 30 percent of total world silver production for the year. The remainder of the total 634.4 million ounces of silver derived from mine production in 2004 (a 4 percent increase over 2003) was a by-product of the mining of copper (26 percent), lead and zinc (32 percent), and gold (12 percent).

Top silver-producing countries in 2004 were Mexico (99.2 million ounces), Peru (98.4 million ounces), Australia (71.9 million ounces), and China (63.8 million ounces). U.S. production of 40.2 million ounces made it the eighth-largest world producer.

Silver supplies from above-ground sources fell from 242.1 million ounces to 202.3 million ounces in 2004, fueled in part by a 30 percent drop in net government sales. (The decline in government sales was due primarily to a steep slide in the amount of silver released from Chinese official stocks—from 61.7 million ounces in 2003 to 34 million ounces in 2004.) Recovery of silver from old silver scrap likewise declined, but only slightly—from 183.6 million ounces to 181.1 million ounces.

Silver ore, like gold, undergoes an extensive process to prepare it for use as an industrial or precious metal. Silver from ore that is relatively free of other mineral contaminants undergoes a cyanide process developed in the late 19th century in which crushed silver ore is added to lime to create an alkaline environment. A solution of water and sodium cyanide is then added to this mixture and various processes are applied to filter off the silver from the solution.

The future production rate of silver depends on the continuing industrial uses of the metal and on potential new uses for silver in fields like medicine. It also depends on the rate of production of metals that produce silver as a by-product.

TRADING

Trading in silver requires that you remain constantly aware of silver supply-and-demand shifts around the world. Silver trading should be done on an exchange where there is significant trading volume and open interest. Needless to say, you should study technical indicators of the price history of silver. The history of silver suggests that prices tend to remain in narrow bands for extended periods of time and periodically break out in sudden and sharp price surges. Consequently, this is a market where speculators have made and lost fortunes. If you wish to speculate in silver, it may be prudent to use stop-losses and/or to hedge your position through options or some other instrument to avoid getting caught on the wrong side of one of those sudden silver price surges. Silver was trading at $9.95 per ounce as of mid-June 2006.

CHAPTER 8

Platinum

OVERVIEW

More valuable than gold, platinum is a chemically inert metallic element that is known for its great resistance to attack by air, water, single acids, and ordinary reagents. Its many uses in industry derive from its ability to withstand high temperatures, acid damage, disintegrating atmospheres, and great stress.

Platinum is heavier than gold and other precious metals and is much rarer. There are platinum mines around the world, but most of the world's concentration of this metal is in South Africa. It takes five months to produce a single troy ounce of pure platinum, and only about 5 million troy ounces of new platinum are produced annually. In fact, all the platinum mined worldwide to date would fit into an average-sized living room.

Because of its strength, rich luster, and resistance to tarnishing agents, platinum is prized by the international jewelry industry, which accounts for about 51 percent of total demand for the metal. Gem settings constitute the single most important jewelry use.

The other primary use of platinum is in auto catalysts, which convert harmful vehicle emissions to less harmful ones. Platinum is also used to produce fiber-optic cable wires, fertilizers, explosives, petrol additives, and anticancer drugs.

This chapter provided courtesy of Johnson Matthey, PLC, Platinum 2005 Interim Review.

Similar to, but less important than, platinum are two related metals—palladium and rhodium. Palladium, which is a by-product of nickel mining, is more common than platinum. Like platinum it is used in automotive catalysts, which accounts for most of its worldwide demand. Rhodium is also used for pollution control devices in the automotive industry.

The most important thing that traders need to keep in mind about the platinum group is how closely its fortunes are tied to the U.S. automotive industry. If Americans are not buying new cars, platinum metals will usually be trading at historic lows.

DEMAND

In the United States, the biggest user of platinum is the auto industry, which represents 60 percent of U.S. consumption, followed by the jewelry industry (25 percent). In both the petroleum and the chemical industries, platinum is used principally as a catalyst. Platinum plays a critical catalytic role in the manufacture of gasoline and of nitric acid and is also used in producing fertilizers, explosives, and plastics. Electrical and electronic uses of platinum include temperature measuring devices and circuit elements. The glass industries use platinum in the manufacture of fiberglass.

Demand for platinum expanded by 2 percent in 2005 to a new high of 6.71 million ounces, fueled in part by a sixth year of increased purchases of platinum for use in auto catalysts. But higher platinum prices resulted in declining purchases by the jewelry industry for the third consecutive year.

Auto catalyst demand for platinum increased by 300,000 ounces in 2005 to reach a total of 3.86 million ounces. The trend of strong annual growth in demand in Europe continued, with automakers in the region purchasing 1.94 million ounces of platinum, up by more than 15 percent compared with 2004. Increased demand from diesel truck manufacturers in Japan, the retrofitting of catalysts to heavy-duty diesel vehicles in the United States, and higher light-vehicle production in Asia also contributed to growth in platinum demand.

In contrast, purchases of platinum for jewelry manufacture declined by just over 6 percent to 2.02 million ounces in 2005. Demand in China dropped for the third year in a row and also weakened in Japan and North America. Higher platinum prices led to a reduction in trade stocks of platinum jewelry and to an increase in the volume of old platinum pieces being recycled.

Demand for platinum in industrial applications grew 5 percent to 1.615 million ounces in 2005. Consumption of the metal in electrical applications increased by 55,000 ounces to 355,000 ounces, thanks to rising production of hard drives. Likewise, demand from glass production increased by almost 9 percent to 315,000 ounces as manufacturers of glass for flat-panel displays continued to invest in new capacity in Asia. In the chemicals sector, however, purchases of platinum softened to 320,000 ounces, with less paraxylene capacity coming on stream in 2005 than in 2004.

Platinum is expected to extend its decade-long demand in the coming years. The auto catalyst market will continue to generate much of the additional demand, with purchases of platinum expected to climb in Europe, North America, and Asia.

Sales of light-duty diesel vehicles in Europe are set to continue to rise, with higher fuel prices reinforcing the advantage of better fuel efficiency that they have over gasoline vehicles. At the same time, the fitting of catalyzed diesel particulate filters (DPF) will increase and thereby push the average platinum loading per vehicle upward. The majority of automakers now offer DPF as optional extras, and one European manufacturer has already begun fitting them as standard equipment.

In North America, new demand from the heavy-duty diesel sector is expected to provide a boost to platinum purchases in coming years. Truck manufacturers serving the U.S. market will begin producing models that comply with strict new emissions legislation, which necessitates the use of diesel oxidation catalysts and, on some vehicles, particulate filters. The impact of this on platinum demand will outweigh by a considerable margin the effects of the ongoing switch to palladium-based catalysts for gasoline light vehicles.

Further growth in platinum demand will stem from higher production of light vehicles in China, India, and Southeast Asia and from the tightening of emissions limits in several major vehicle markets.

In contrast, in the current price environment, jewelry demand for platinum will remain vulnerable. A further contraction in stocks held by retailers and an increase in recycling is probable in China. There is also the possibility that growth in retail sales of palladium jewelry may occur partly at the expense of platinum.

The outlook for purchases of platinum for jewelry in other markets is also uncertain. It is possible that demand in Europe, Japan, and North America will stabilize at current levels; but platinum will continue to face strong competition from other white metals.

The prognosis for the use of platinum in industrial applications is positive. Further growth in production of hard disks and additional investment in new LCD (liquid crystal display) glass manufacturing plants in Asia should see demand from the electrical and glass sectors rise again; and consumption of the metal in catalysts for the chemicals industry is also forecast to increase, primarily due to investment in new manufacturing capacity in China.

SUPPLY

Supplies of platinum rose by 2 percent to 6.59 million ounces in 2005. South African supplies of platinum increased by 150,000 ounces in 2005 to total 5.12 million ounces. Output would have been higher but for the closure of Anglo Platinum's smelter in Polokwane for repairs following an explosion in September. For Anglo Platinum, the world's largest platinum producer, the incident resulted in refined platinum output falling short of the company's target for the year of 2.6 million ounces.

Platinum output from the world's second largest producer, Impala Platinum Holdings, on the western limb of the Bushveld Complex in South Africa, increased by 4 percent during the first half of 2005, thanks to increased productivity and higher mill throughput, and was on course to exceed 1.1 million ounces of platinum production for the second year in a row. The rate of development at the company's Marula mine on the eastern Bushveld, however, has been constrained by the need to switch from mechanized to conventional mining methods.

Lonmin PLC's production of platinum fell by 11 percent during the first half of 2005 to 457,000 ounces, largely due to the depletion of shallow UG2 reserves, a platinum-bearing reef in the Northwest Province of South Africa. However, the company's output during the second half of 2005 received a boost from the refining of pipeline stocks of metal that accumulated following a smelter shutdown in late 2004.

Shipments of platinum from Russia in 2005 totaled 860,000 ounces, marginally higher than in 2004. Russian's largest platinum producer, Norilsk Nickel, published data on its output of platinum and palladium for the first time in September 2005, revealing that it had produced 355,000 ounces of platinum in the first six months of 2005 and estimating output for the full year of 730,000 ounces. Production from the alluvial operations in the far east of Russia slipped lower in 2005, while sales of the metal from state stocks were minimal.

North American supplies of platinum fell to an estimated 340,000 ounces in 2005. Sales by Inco Ltd. declined due to the temporary closure of its smelter for scheduled maintenance, and production from North American Palladium dropped in line with reduced palladium output. Shipments of platinum from Zimbabwe, however, increased by 5 percent to 155,000 ounces as a result of higher production at both the Ngezi and Mimosa mines.

As with demand, supplies of platinum are set to grow in the coming years, barring any further disruptions to production in South Africa. The ongoing expansion of mining operations should deliver a greater increase in refined platinum output. South Africa will remain the world's largest producer, and mining operations there bear close watching in order to determine world supply in any given year.

North American output should also improve in 2006, and production in Zimbabwe is likely to continue growing slowly. Russian sales of platinum are forecast to be maintained at or close to the rate of mine production.

Supplies of platinum and demand for the metal are projected to grow at similar rates in the near future, and the market is therefore set to remain in deficit. With fund interest in precious metals still high and the fundamentals supportive, the price of platinum could trade significantly higher. On the downside, it is hard to imagine platinum prices falling below $890 unless demand from jewelry manufacturers contracts more substantially than current trends suggest.

TRADING

During the first nine months of 2005, supplies of platinum increased but failed to keep pace with strong growth in demand. The availability of metal, however, was not excessively tight, with short-term lease rates typically being quoted in the 3 to 6 percent range. The primary stimulus to the price came from the speculative side of the market, with funds building record long positions.

To give a sense of the forces that move the platinum market, the following is a summation of the price action for the first nine month of 2005. Those who wish to speculate in platinum can see that a number of factors impact platinum prices and that it is important to remain flexible in response to changing supply-and-demand dynamics.

The platinum price began 2005 weakly, sliding from around $860 at the end of 2004 to $843 on January 5. However, good physical demand soon appeared from industrial end users and Chinese jewelry manufacturers—and, as the U.S. dollar weakened against the yen, significant buying was seen from Tokyo Commodities Exchange (TOCOM) investors. With U.S.–based funds also increasing their long exposure, the platinum price rose steadily, ending January trading either side of $870.

The rally continued in Asia on February 1, 2005, as a burst of short covering on TOCOM pushed the spot price up to $881. At this level, bids for metal were scaled back, with demand from Chinese buyers dwindling as the Chinese New Year holiday approached. At the same time, the dollar recovered against the yen, triggering selling by Japanese investors. As a result, by February 9, platinum had dropped to $847. The dip encouraged renewed speculative buying, and the price recovered to trade between $856 and $877 through to the end of the month.

The price climbed unevenly during the first half of March as funds continued to add to long positions, platinum fixing at $883 on March 16 and 17. The precious metals markets then reversed direction as the dollar strengthened again and platinum fell to hit $858 on March 23. The price subsequently traded quietly between $855 and $865 through to April 19, supported by firm physical demand.

Funds then became more active, and the platinum price rallied to $880 on April 26. At that point the net speculative position on the New York Mercantile Exchange (NYMEX) had risen to just over 320,000 ounces, up from less than 260,000 ounces two weeks earlier. As in March, the move to $880 sparked long liquidation, and the price consequently eased back to end the month at $867.

Additional fund buying took the price up to $881 on the May 11. However, once again the move above $880 was swiftly followed by a fall, with platinum sliding to $853 on May 16. The long liquidation was part of a broader sell-off, with gold, base metal, and oil prices all dropping as funds continued to trade commodities against the dollar. Bids from end users picked up below $860, and platinum recovered to trade between $858 and $868 from May 18 onward.

Platinum remained range-bound until June 15, when a sudden reversal in the value of the dollar drew a surge of fund buying into the metals and oil markets. Platinum fixed at $877 in London that afternoon, passed $890 on June 17, and reached $900 on June 20 as the dollar weakened. By that stage, the net speculative position on the NYMEX had leapt to almost 400,000 ounces, up from little more than 200,000 ounces at the beginning of the month. Platinum slipped back to fix at $879 on the June 21 in the face of fund profit taking but then recovered to trade between $880 and $895 for the remainder of June.

Early July 2005 saw another round of long liquidation in the metals markets as the dollar recovered some ground. As a result, the platinum price dropped back into its previous trading range of $860 to $880. The announcement by the Chinese government of a revaluation of the *renminbi* (a 100-yuan note) on July 21, however, immediately spurred increased fund buying of commodities, particularly those for which China accounts for a substantial proportion of physical demand. The platinum price moved swiftly above $880 and had reached $898 by the afternoon of July 29.

The rally continued into the first half of August, short-covering by individual investors on TOCOM contributing to the upward momentum. The price moved above $900 on August 1 and hit $914 on August 4. After a brief round of profit taking, platinum ran up to $924 at the morning fixing on August 12 as the precious metals markets moved up in parallel with a surge in the price of crude oil. At that point, the net speculative position on the NYMEX had passed 460,000 ounces—the highest level for almost six years.

Increased offers of metal then came forward, and the rally began to falter, end users being largely absent from the market. Funds started taking profits, and by the close of trading on August 16, platinum had retreated to $887. Nevertheless, sentiment remained bullish, and platinum continued to trade firmly either side of $890 through to the end of the month.

Precious metals markets continued to attract fresh fund investment in September. Platinum jumped from $893 on September 1 to $909 the next day as the dollar weakened amid the aftermath of Hurricane Katrina. The metal was supported around that level through to September 15 before embarking on another strong rally as the price of gold surged from less than $450 toward $470. Platinum passed $920 on September 19 and hit $930 the following day as short-covering on TOCOM intensified. By that stage, the net speculative position on the NYMEX had soared to just over 507,000 ounces; but physical demand, particularly from the Chinese jewelry sector, was minimal. After easing back to $910 on September 28 in the face of profit taking, platinum rebounded to end the third quarter at $929, a rise of nearly 10 percent from the opening fixing of the year. At June 15, 2006, platinum was trading at $1,160 per ounce on strong buying by hedge funds.

CHAPTER 9

Copper

OVERVIEW

It is estimated that copper, the oldest metal ever utilized, was discovered 10,000 years ago. Archeologists have found copper smelting sites that date back to about 4500 BCE in present-day Jordan, Egypt, and Israel. Still serviceable copper tubing used for plumbing can be found in the temples and tombs of ancient Egypt.

Copper is considered a "half" precious metal, and its reddish hue makes it the only metal other than gold to be colored. It occurs as a solid and in minerals. The primary deposits for this metal are in Chile and the United States.

Tough, flexible, and relatively hard, copper has good chemical stability. This makes copper ideally suitable for the production of very thin lamellas and fine wires. When exposed to air, copper mixes with basic sulfates, carbonates, and chloride to form a greenish patina that protects the copper from further corrosion.

Its strong erosion-resistant properties and excellent ability to conduct electricity make copper one of the most widely used metals in industry. Refined copper, the final product from the treatment of concentrates, is incorporated into wire and cable products for use in the construction, electric utility, communications, and transportation industries. Copper is also used in industrial equipment and machinery, consumer products, and a variety of other electrical and electronic applications.

Copper is combined with zinc to make brass and with tin to make bronze, both of which are harder metals than pure copper. And because bacteria will not grow on its surface, copper plays an important role in helping to prevent the spread of diseases.

Copper substitutes include aluminum, plastics, stainless steel, and fiber optics. Refined, or cathode, copper is also an internationally traded commodity.

Because the demand for copper is sensitive to the overall level of economic activity, any deep recession invariably results in a sharp decline in copper prices, and any strong upsurge in economic activity results in significant price increases in the metal. So a long-term graph of copper prices displays sharp increases and decreases, which are roughly in concert with economic activity.

DEMAND

World demand for copper was forecast to rise to 14.98 million tons in 2005, an increase of about 460,000 tons, according to the International Copper Study Group (ICSG), an organization consisting of government delegates and industry officials from most of the world copper producing and using countries. The ICSG forecasts world copper demand to increase 5.5 percent in 2007 to 17.36 million tons.

The increased world demand in 2006 will be largely a function of strong economic growth in China, India, and other Asian nations. The ICSG forecasts that total Asian demand will rise to 7.63 million tons in 2006 from 7.1 million tons in 2005. Smaller increases in demand are forecast for North America (3.0 million tons in 2006 compared to 2.89 million tons in 2005) and for the European Union (3.9 million tons in 2006 compared to 3.76 in 2005).

In the United States, the breakdown of copper usage is:

Building construction: 49%
Electrical products: 21%
Transportation equipment: 11%
Industrial machinery and equipment: 9%
Consumer and other products: 10%

The bulk of copper consumption in the United States occurs at about 30 brass mills, 15 rod mills, and 500 foundries, chemical plants, and other manufacturing facilities. Brass mills account for about 74 percent of U.S. copper usage.

SUPPLY

The ICSG forecasts that world copper mine production is expected to increased to about 14.98 million tons in 2005, a rise of about 460,000 tons from 2004. Supply disruptions in Chile and the United States resulted in a smaller production increase in 2005 than was anticipated by analysts going into the year.

In 2006, the ICSG projects world mine production of 15.74 million tons, a further increase of 760,000 tons. The bulk of the increased production is forecast to come from Chile and the United States, as the production disruptions of 2005 are not expected to be repeated in 2006.

As a result of the increased production in 2006, the ICSG forecasts that supply will exceed demand worldwide by about 300,000 tons. In 2005, demand exceeded production by 120,000 tons and in 2004, demand exceeded production by 800,000 tons.

TRADING

Copper futures and options are traded on the Commodity Exchange (COMEX) Division of the New York Mercantile Exchange and the London Metal Exchange. Copper futures are also traded on the Shanghai Futures Exchange. The COMEX futures contract calls for delivery of 25,000 pounds of Grade 1 electrolytic copper. Price changes are registered in multiples of five one-hundredths of one cent (0.05 cents or $0.0005) per pound, equivalent to $12.50 per contract. A fluctuation of one cent is equivalent to $250 per contract.

Copper prices have rallied substantially since hitting a low of about 60 cents per pound in 2001. Since then, the price has nearly quadrupled, rising to about $2.25 in early 2006. Although it's anticipated that supply will increase in the years to come—mitigating upward price pressures—it is expected that demand from China, India, and other rapidly growing economies will increase substantially. That being the case, prices are likely to be very sensitive to supply disruptions and global economic growth trends.

Copper was trading at $3.30 per pound at June 15, 2006. This high price level led to discussions of substituting more inexpensive materials, such as plastics, in place of copper piping in plumbing. Copper is currently trading at about four times what it traded in 2001 and it is trading at levels 50 percent higher than at the beginning of 2001, on continuing demand from India and China.

CHAPTER 10

Palladium

OVERVIEW

Palladium is one of the platinum group metals (PGM), which also include rhodium, iridium, osmium, and ruthenium. Like platinum, these metals are resistant to erosion and, to some extent, can replace platinum and each other in industrial applications.

Palladium is a white, malleable metal that at room temperatures can absorb up to 900 times its own volume of hydrogen, which uniquely qualifies palladium as a medium for purifying the gas. Palladium and platinum are generally mined together, but palladium is less rare than platinum because it is also a by-product of nickel mining.

Palladium is primarily used in automotive catalyst production, which accounts for 63 percent of total demand. To a lesser extent, palladium is also used in electronic equipment, dental alloys, and jewelry.

Rhodium is also mainly used in pollution control devices for the automotive industry. Likewise, iridium is used in some automotive catalysts as well as in the production of polyvinyl chloride. These two metals are covered next in Chapter 11.

This chapter provided courtesy of Johnson Matthey, PLC, Platinum 2005 Interim Review.

DEMAND

Demand for palladium rose by about 410,000 ounces to 6.89 million ounces in 2005. Most of the growth was due to a surge in purchases of the metal for the manufacture of jewelry.

Purchases of palladium for the manufacture of jewelry soared to 1.43 million ounces, an increase of more than 500,000 ounces compared with 2004. Almost all of the growth stemmed from increased production of palladium jewelry in China. Purchases of palladium for jewelry manufacture in China jumped by a remarkable 71 percent to 1.20 million ounces this year, as the trade pipeline continues to fill and retail sales develop.

For jewelry manufacturers, the much lower metal costs associated with palladium compared to platinum and the relative stability of the palladium price are major advantages. Palladium has expanded the market for white precious metal jewelry in China by offering less affluent consumers a high purity but relatively affordable product. For retailers in China, palladium jewelry has the additional benefit of carrying significantly higher profit margins per piece than platinum. As a result, the numbers of stores stocking palladium and the amount of counter space apportioned to it have increased.

How the market continues to develop will depend upon numerous factors, including the amount of promotion undertaken, the price of the metal, and whether it becomes available to trade on the Shanghai Gold Exchange. On balance, jewelry demand for palladium has the potential to increase further in the coming years; but as expansion of the trade pipeline is expected to slow, the rate of growth is forecast to be much less dramatic than in 2005.

Demand from the electronics sector rose to about 970,000 ounces on the back of greater use of the metal in plating solutions, whereas consumption in other applications was broadly stable. The use of palladium in most other applications, including dental alloys and catalysts for chemicals manufacture, rose slightly.

Auto catalyst demand for palladium fell by about 1 percent to 3.69 million ounces in 2005. The effects of lower-gasoline-usage vehicle output in Europe and thrifting in the United States outweighed greater purchases in Asia.

Looking ahead, auto catalyst demand for palladium is forecast to return to growth. The ongoing move away from platinum-based auto catalysts to those using palladium in North America should have a more substantial effect on purchases of the metal, while the negative effect of thrifting is expected to diminish.

In Japan, auto catalyst demand for palladium is also projected to expand as a greater proportion of light vehicles produced for both the domestic and European markets meet more stringent emissions limits. Purchases of palladium for auto catalysts in China and elsewhere in Asia will continue to rise as light-vehicle output grows but will decline again in Europe as diesels gain additional market share.

SUPPLY

Sales of Russian palladium declined by about 9 percent to 3.73 million ounces in 2005, with little metal being supplied by Gokhran or the Central Bank. This total includes 438,000 ounces of metal that was sold from stocks held by Stillwater Mining in the United States. Shipments of platinum and rhodium in 2005 from Russia were 860,000 ounces and 90,000 ounces respectively.

Norilsk Nickel revealed its production of platinum and palladium for the first time in September 2005, stating that it had produced 1.483 million ounces of palladium and 355,000 ounces of platinum in the first six months of 2005. Sales were slightly below production levels, at 1.469 million ounces of palladium and 327,000 ounces of platinum. Full-year production was forecast at 3.08 million ounces of palladium and 730,000 ounces of platinum.

The 2005 Russian supply figure for palladium includes material sold by Stillwater Mining from the 877,169 ounces transferred in 2003 by Norilsk Nickel in part payment for a majority shareholding in the company. Although the metal was exported from Russia in 2003, none was sold during that year; and so it was not included in our supply data. Early in 2004, Stillwater entered into agreements to sell palladium at a rate of approximately 36,500 ounces per month from this stock.

Meanwhile, South African production should increase significantly. In June 2005, Lonmin PLC completed the acquisition of Southern Platinum, owner of the Messina platinum project. The Messina lease area currently hosts one mine, Voorspoed, which produced around 45,000 ounces of platinum in 2004. Lonmin intends to proceed with an expansion to raise annual output to 75,000 ounces by 2007.

Following a difficult 2004, production at Northam recovered strongly in the first six months of this year, with platinum output rising 12 percent to 109,000 ounces. Mill throughput was up 14 percent, largely due to a sharp increase in tonnage from the UG2 reef. There was also an improvement

---

*In this discussion, Troy ounces and metric tons are used. (32,000 Troy ounces = 1 metric ton.)

in Merensky production, although geological conditions remained very difficult. The average head grade declined slightly, in line with the change in the ore mix; but this was offset by an improvement in recoveries from the UG2 ore.

In addition to its Kroondal and Marikana operations, both of which are the subject of agreements with Anglo Platinum, Aquarius Platinum has a third South African platinum mine currently under development at Everest South. A 250,000-ton-per-month concentrator was commissioned in December 2005. The initial feed for the concentrator will come from two small open pits before mining subsequently moves underground. At full production, Everest South is planned to produce 225,000 ounces of PGM annually.

ARM Platinum is involved in three PGM-producing joint ventures: It currently holds a 41.5 percent stake in Modikwa (joint venture with Anglo Platinum), 50 percent of the Nkomati nickel mine (with LionOre), and 55 percent of the Two Rivers project (with Impala).

In June 2005, ARM and Impala Platinum confirmed their decision to proceed with the Two Rivers PGM project, following a successful trial mining operation. Production is due to start in the second half of 2006, with a stockpile of around 300,000 tons of UG2 ore already having been established. At full capacity, the operation is scheduled to produce 120,000 ounces of platinum, 68,000 ounces of palladium, and 20,000 ounces of rhodium annually.

The Nkomati nickel mine reported higher sales of by-product PGM in the first half of this year, up 8 percent to 18,000 ounces. ARM Platinum and LionOre are currently evaluating an expansion that would more than triple nickel production at Nkomati; the increase in PGM output would be proportionately slightly less.

North American supplies of PGM declined in 2005 due to lower production from both Inco and North American Palladium. Platinum shipments totalled 340,000 ounces, down 12 percent compared with 2004, while sales of palladium declined by 11 percent to 925,000 ounces.

The Lac des Iles open-pit mine operated by North American Palladium had a difficult start to 2005. The operation produced 101,000 ounces of palladium in concentrate in the first six months of the year, 60 percent less than the same period in 2004. Problems with mill availability and a fall in palladium head grades to less than 2 grams per ton were key factors in the drop in output. An underground mine is currently under development at Lac des Iles. This will exploit deeper reserves grading over 6 grams per ton of palladium and should therefore lift overall head grades when it enters production in early 2006.

By-product PGM output from nickel-copper mines in Canada also decreased in 2005. Following a scheduled shutdown of its smelter for maintenance and upgrading, Inco Ltd.'s PGM production totaled around 380,000 ounces in 2005, compared with 422,000 ounces in 2004. At Falconbridge's Sudbury operations, PGM output in 2005 was similar to 2004, but production from Raglan dropped a little in line with lower nickel and PGM grades.

At Stillwater Mining's operations in Montana, PGM production fell slightly in the first half of 2005. The company's total mill throughput was almost unchanged, but there were declines in grade at both the Stillwater and the East Boulder mines. As a result, palladium output dropped 4 percent to 218,000 ounces in the six months to June 2005, while platinum production slipped 3 percent to 65,000 ounces.

Finally, production of platinum in Zimbabwe rose by 5 percent to 155,000 ounces in 2005. Further increases should be seen in coming years as an upgrade of the Mimosa Mine comes online. However, a planned expansion at Ngezi has been put on hold until political and economic conditions improve.

At the Ngezi mine, owned by Zimplats (in which Impala has an 87 percent share), mill throughput in the first half of 2005 was steady at 1.03 million tons. However, an increasing proportion of this ore came from underground, contributing to improvements in head grades and recoveries. As a result, production of PGM in concentrate rose by 5 percent to 90,000 ounces.

At the Mimosa mine (a joint venture between Impala and Aquarius), a strong increase in mill throughput and an increase in the average head grade during the first half of the year more than offset a slight decrease in recoveries. Production of PGM in concentrate rose by 20 percent to 69,000 ounces as a result. In October 2005, work commenced on a project that will increase mill throughput by a further 25 percent and expand the mine's annual rate of production to nearly 170,000 ounces of PGM by mid-2006.

TRADING

After five years of significant surpluses, the palladium market could move close to balance in 2006 and 2007. Market stocks of metal, however, remain substantial; and so the direction of the price will continue to rest largely with speculative funds. The improving fundamentals of the palladium market should keep sentiment positive and may draw in sufficient additional speculative investment to push the price upward, particularly if gold and platinum also rally. Palladium was trading at $400 per ounce at June 15, 2006, as Chinese jewelry manufacturers had begun substituting it for the more expensive platinum in their manufacturing operations.

PART FOUR

Speculating in Energy

CHAPTER 11

Crude Oil

OVERVIEW

It does not take an oil analyst to assess the state of the energy sector. Anyone who drives a car or pays heating bills is intimately familiar with what is happening: Dwindling supplies and increasing demand are driving energy prices higher. The problem can only get worse. There is just so much crude oil in the world, and it is estimated that 90 percent of the world's oil has already been found. As Matthew R. Simmons succinctly stated in his groundbreaking analysis of the oil industry, *Twilight in the Desert* (Wiley, 2006), "Sooner or later, the worldwide use of oil must peak because oil, like the other two fossil fuels—coal and natural gas—is nonrenewable." Already oil companies are identifying oil reserves at a much lower rate than nations are consuming them.

The other concern is politically sensitive suppliers such as Venezuela and Nigeria. In such regions, production can be curtailed overnight.

Current consumption levels suggest that the world's oil supply should last until around 2045. The impact of depletion will hit much sooner than midcentury, however. "The issue is not about finally running out of oil," noted Colin Campbell, chairman and founder of the Association for the Study of Peak Oil, at a 2005 conference in Edinburgh, Scotland. "What does concern us gravely is the long downward slope that opens on the other side of peak production. Oil and gas dominate our lives, and their decline will change the world in radical and unpredictable ways."

That change is already being felt. There used to be an old adage in the oil business: "You make your money on exploration and operate your marketing at breakeven." The strategy worked well enough prior to energy shocks such as the 1973 Arab oil embargo, the 1976 creation of the Organization of the Petroleum Exporting Countries (OPEC), and the 1981 decontrol of petroleum prices.

In subsequent decades, however, oil companies discovered that profitability from exploration was no longer guaranteed. Petroleum marketers were forced to pay close attention to changes in supply and demand as well.

Both oil supply and demand are closely linked to price changes, which is to say they are somewhat price elastic. As prices climb, consumption declines, while production becomes more cost effective and supply increases. Likewise, when prices drop, consumption rises and production shrinks. With oil, however, there is usually a lag in the response of consumption to price fluctuations. High gas prices, for example, have finally soured demand for the once popular SUV (sport utility vehicle); but it will take many months for Detroit to retool plants for the production of smaller, more energy-efficient models that will reduce consumption.

The shrinking pool of world oil reserves has accelerated a search for alternative energy sources. But the sheer magnitude of the world's energy dependence—oil makes up 90 percent of the world's current energy consumption—means that it will require a considerable period of time to make this transition as well.

As oil reserves become more precarious, look for prices of petroleum products to fluctuate widely in response to changing supply-and-demand fundamentals in the energy sector—a scenario that should present commodity markets with significant trading opportunities. But beginning traders must keep in mind that risk and volatility go hand in hand—the more extreme a market's volatility, the greater its potential risks.

DEMAND

Over the past 30 years, daily oil consumption has risen by approximately 33 million barrels. Asia has accounted for more than half of this growth in demand, which could climb considerably as Asians' love for the automobile grows. Some expect that over the next 10 to 15 years, China will have some 150 million automobiles on the road, the same as in America now. If this is the case, experts project that the world oil consumption will jump from 80 million barrels a day currently to 110 barrels of a day for the next 10 to 15 years.

SUPPLY

World crude production hit a record high of 72.5 million barrels per day in 2004 (*CRB Commodity Yearbook 2005* estimate). The world's largest producers were Saudi Arabia (13 percent of world production), Russia (12 percent), the United States (7 percent), Iran (6 percent), and China (5 percent). U.S. crude production of 5.43 million barrels was a 4 percent decline from 2003, however, and the country's lowest production level in some three decades.

Although final figures were not available when this book was written, U.S. production totals were lower than historical levels in 2005 due to hurricane damage to drilling platforms in the Gulf of Mexico. The Gulf Coast region provides about 29 percent of the country's oil production, and many oil rigs remained shut down months after hurricanes Katrina and Rita hit the coast in August and September of 2005 (see Table 11.1).

Growth in world oil production will be limited in the coming decade. An increasing number of key world oil producers have either peaked or are approaching a peak in their ability to produce oil, constraining the potential for future increases in supplies. As countries with rapidly growing industrial sectors drive up oil consumption, experts anticipate that demand for oil could outstrip supplies within the next five years.

TABLE 11.1 Refineries Impacted by Hurricane Katrina

Company	Refinery	Capacity (bpd)
ChevronTexaco	Pascagoula, MS	325,000
ConocoPhillips	Belle Chasse, LA	247,000
ExxonMobil	Chalmette, LA	187,000
ExxonMobil	Baton Rouge, LA	493,500
Marathon	Garyville, LA	245,000
Murphy	Meraux, LA	120,000
Royal Dutch/Motiva	Convent, LA	235,000
Royal Dutch/Motiva	Norco, LA	227,000
Valero Energy	St. Charles, LA	260,000
Valero Energy	Krotz Springs, LA	85,000
Premcor	Memphis, TN	190,000
Total		2,614,500

TRADING

The oil market is a two-tier market—a *contract market* and a *spot market*. As prices of petroleum products fluctuate widely in response to supply-and-demand fundamentals, buyers and sellers engage in a protracted struggle to obtain fixed-price, 18-month contracts as a means of insulating themselves from the price swings. The oil-futures contract market covers 90 percent of the product being distributed, with the spot market accounting for the balance. The petroleum spot market works like any spot market: If a supplier runs out of product from his or her contracted source, he or she purchases it from another source at a premium.

As the futures contract month approaches its expiration, the futures price tends to approach or "converge" on the cash price. If there is a difference in the cash and futures prices, the possibility for arbitrage exists. Earlier we looked at a "cash-and-carry" trading technique that flows from this—if the cash price is below the futures price by more than the cost of carrying the product until delivery, you would buy the cash product, sell the futures, and deliver the product to close out the futures contract against payment.

These are pretty basic trading principles, but you cannot afford to forget them. And if you need protection from rising prices, you would use a long hedge. Here, for example, you might want to sign a contract with a consumer at a fixed price to be determined at delivery time. You would buy futures contracts (the "long hedge") equivalent to your delivery commitment. Come delivery time, you would purchase product in the spot market; and the only loss experienced would be made up when you liquidated your long position.

Some of the biggest traders in the oil futures markets are refining companies, of which there are a limited number: Chevron/Texaco, ConocoPhillips, ExxonMobil, Marathon, Murphy, Royal Dutch/Motiva, Valero Energy, and Premcor. These refineries make use of the trading technique known as "spreading," the simultaneous purchase and sale of different contract months.

Here is how spreading works. The price differences between months represent both the costs of carrying product (storage, insurance, finance) for the period between deliveries as well as the market's expectations about the futures product prices. When futures delivery months show successive premiums, the market is said to be a carrying charge market. When the near months gain on the distant months and eventually trade at a premium to the deferred contracts, this is known as an inverted market, or "backwardation."

Generally, if supplies of crude or gasoline or heating oil or natural gas become tight, as when Hurricane Katrina disrupted crude oil and natural gas production in the Gulf of Mexico, traders will bid up the front months as they seek to obtain the commodity immediately, before prices escalate. When supplies are plentiful (and we may never return to this scenario in the energy complex), commodity-trading markets will exhibit some or all of the carrying costs.

The changing relationships between contract markets should be monitored closely, for they can be used to the trader's benefit. When choosing a month to trade, traders should be aware of both their own marketing needs and the spread differences between contract months.

Another trading technique is "arbitrage," the simultaneous purchase and sale of contracts in two different physical markets. Arbitrage is similar to spreading.

Finally, the most important element to a successful trading strategy is a thorough knowledge and familiarity with basis. *Basis* is defined as the price difference between the cash commodity at a given delivery point and the nearby or a distant future. In simple terms, basis is the price of the cash commodity versus the futures price, or the spread between cash and futures prices.

Usually, the basis value will depend upon the cost of storage, insurance, and financing charges for the cash commodity over a given period. Differences in location and product, however, may also be factored into a basis calculation. If a user is hedging heating oil or gasoline with a different sulfur content or octane rating than the one that is specified in the contract, the price fluctuations of that particular grade may not match exactly the futures price—the basis may either narrow or widen somewhat.

The principles involved in utilizing changing cash and futures relationships are similar to those the hedger would apply to changing spread relationships. If a dealer holds inventory and sells futures as a hedge, he or she is "long the basis." The dealer will then profit if spot prices rise more than futures prices or if futures prices decline more than spot oil. When the dealer is obligated to deliver product and purchases futures against his or her short inventory position, then the dealer is "short the basis." If futures advance more than spot oil prices, the distributor receives an additional profit on the futures side of the hedge.

Crude oil is the most actively traded commodity world. Futures of crude oil trade on the New York Mercantile Exchange (NYMEX) and the International Petroleum Exchange (IPE) in London. Two main types of crude oil trade on the NYMEX: light sweet crude oil and Brent crude oil. Refineries prefer the light sweet crude oil because it has low sulfur content and yields a large volume of high-value products such as gasoline and heating oil. Brent crude is based on light sweet North Sea crude oil.

The NYMEX futures contract for light sweet crude oil calls for delivery of 1,000 barrels (42,000 gallons) of crude oil to be delivered to Cushing,

Oklahoma. It is the most liquid forum for crude oil trading and the world's largest-volume futures contract trading on a physical commodity. Its liquidity and price transparency make it a popular international pricing benchmark.

Price quotations for NYMEX futures contracts are in U.S. dollars and cents per barrel. The maximum daily price fluctuation is $10 per barrel (i.e., $10,000 per contract) for all months. Crude oil was trading at $69.50 per barrel as of mid-June 2006.

CHAPTER 12

Gasoline

OVERVIEW

Gasoline, a complex mix of hydrocarbons, is the biggest product derived from crude petroleum. Refineries convert more than half of every barrel of crude produced into gasoline in a three-part process that separates crude into chemical components, breaks down chemicals into molecules (hydrocarbons), and transforms and combines hydrocarbons with other additives.

Gasoline is the single-largest-volume refined product sold in the United States, and total gas usage represents 17 percent of the energy consumed in this country. Its market is large and diverse. Some 168,987 retail outlets offer gasoline to the consumer in three octane grades of unleaded fuel (octane measures gasoline's ability to resist engine knocking). This extremely diverse market is also very competitive and is subject to intense price volatility.

The Clean Air Act of 1990 required that ethanol be added to unleaded gasoline to reduce harmful emissions. Currently, some 2 billion gallons of ethanol—an alcohol-based fuel—are added to gasoline in the United States each year. The most common blend of gasoline and ethanol is 90 percent gasoline and 10 percent ethanol.

DEMAND

Gasoline consumption is growing worldwide, especially in countries with fast-growing economies, such as China and India. Global demand for petroleum, for example, grew 3.4 percent in 2004, or about 2.7 million barrels per day, with China representing 38.9 percent of the increase. Current worldwide consumption of oil products is 84 million barrels per day.

Growth in U.S. demand for gasoline has been less than that of developing nations, but total demand nonetheless climbed to a record-high 9.054 million gallons per day in 2004 (data through November, annualized *CRB Commodity Yearbook 2005*). That was a gain of 1.3 percent over 2003 consumption levels.

Indeed, the United States is the biggest consumer of gasoline in the world, with gas representing nearly half of the country's total petroleum consumption. Analysts project that U.S. demand for motor gasoline will continue to grow in 2006 and 2007, increasing 1.7 percent per year.

SUPPLY

U.S. production of gasoline rose 2.1 percent in 2004 to 8.678 million barrels per day (data through November, annualized *CRB Commodity Yearbook 2005*). By early 2006, gasoline stocks had recovered from their lows of about 195 million barrels in the wake of the 2005 hurricanes to just under 220 million barrels. Analysts project inventories to range between 200 and 225 million barrels in 2006.

Gasoline refiners in the United States have adopted increasingly efficient technologies and business strategies in recent years, allowing them to produce more gasoline from each barrel of crude they process. Different regions in the United States have varying access to gasoline supplies, however, which can drive up prices in one area relative to another. For example, prices on the East Coast, in the Midwest, and in the Rockies are generally much more variable than prices in the Gulf Coast region, where there is typically excess refining capacity.

The Organization of Petroleum Exporting Countries (OPEC) oil production—according to the Energy Information Administration—will rise to 33.3 million barrels per day by 2010 if oil prices are high and to 42.8 million barrels per day if oil prices are low.

TRADING

The most heavily used risk-management tool in regional and national gasoline markets is the New York Mercantile Exchange (NYMEX) Division New York Harbor unleaded gasoline futures contract. These contracts trade in units of one barrel (42,000 gallons) and are based on delivery at petroleum products terminals in New York harbor, the major East Coast trading center for imports and domestic shipments from refineries.

New York Harbor unleaded gasoline futures contracts trade every calendar month, from January through December. Price quotations for these contracts are in U.S. dollars and cents per barrel. The maximum price fluctuation is $0.25 per gallon ($10,500 per contract) for all months. Gasoline was trading at $2.01 per gallon at mid-June 2006.

The contract specifications conform to those for reformulated gasoline, required in many areas for controlling emissions that can adversely affect air quality. To ensure that the terms and conditions of the gasoline futures contract continue to mirror the cash market, NYMEX maintains close contact with federal and state officials and continues to evaluate changes in government regulations.

The government is also evaluating alternative fuels, such as ethanol (extracted from corn), to reduce the country's dependence on oil imports from the Middle East, as well as reducing pollutants in the environment. Retailer Wal-Mart is pilot testing ethanol-based fuels at its service stations and most of the vehicles on the road in Brazil now run on ethanol. In our country, the largest ethanol producer is Archer Daniels Midland.

CHAPTER 13

Heating Oil

OVERVIEW

Heating oil, a heavy fuel oil, represents 25 percent of the yield from a barrel of oil. For this reason, heating oil is also known as *Number two oil*, second to gasoline, which represents about 50 percent of the yield from a barrel of oil. As is the case with gasoline, heating oil prices are closely correlated to those of crude oil.

About 8.1 million of the 107 million households rely on heating oil as their primary means of home heat, a number that reflects a significant decline over the past three decades as many households have turned to heating alternatives like natural gas. The American Petroleum Institute reports that demand for heating oil is down some 10 billion gallons per year from its 1979 peak. The Northeastern and Central Atlantic states are those most reliant on heating oil.

The United States produces about 85 percent of its heating oil. The rest is imported from Canada, the Virgin Islands, and Venezuela. Recent innovations in heating oil alternatives include substituting 20 percent of fuel oil with soybean oil, an additive that could save 1.3 billion gallons in fuel oil annually.

DEMAND

The biggest determinant of domestic heating oil demand is the weather. A rapid change to cold weather can deplete heating oil supplies more quickly than anticipated, putting pressure on refineries, delivery systems, and remaining supplies, which drives up prices.

Usage of U.S. distillate fuel oil rose 3.3 percent to a new record high of 4.056 million barrels per day in 2004 (through November, annualized *CRB Commodity Yearbook 2005*). These figures include both heating fuel and diesel fuel usage.

SUPPLY

The two sources of heating oil for the United States are domestic refineries and imports from other countries. Refineries produce heating oil as part of a distillate fuel oil product family, which includes diesel oil as well as heating oil. As noted previously, most U.S. imports of distillate fuel oil are from Canada, the Virgin Islands, and Venezuela.

Domestic refineries are limited as to how much distillate they can produce. This is because in order to significantly increase production of heating oil, they would have to increase production of other petroleum products as well—products that cannot be sold in sufficient quantities during the winter months. To ease this problem, refineries produce some heating oil in the summer and fall months and store it as a backup to help meet unexpected winter demand. Even so, supply imbalances can occur, driving up short-term heating oil prices.

U.S. production of distillate fuel oil in 2004 rose 2.3 percent year over year to 3,792 million barrels per day (through November, annualized *CRB Commodity Yearbook 2005*). Domestic production of residual fuel fell 2.4 percent (through November, annualized *CRB Commodity Yearbook 2005*) year over year to 644,000 barrels per day. And U.S. stocks of residual fuel had risen to 37.5 million barrels by July 2004, compared with 35.3 million barrels a year earlier.

TRADING

The New York Mercantile Exchange (NYMEX) introduced the world's first successful energy contract in 1978 to take advantage of increasing volatility in the energy market. At first, mainly wholesalers and large consumers of heating oil in the New York area used the contract. Eventually, its use spread beyond New York, and it was used as a hedge for diesel fuel as well. Now participants in a variety of oil-related industries use the contract as a tool for managing risk. The fact that the contracts trade for 18 consecutive months means that traders can execute strategies that will apply to two winters.

The NYMEX Division heating oil contract can also be used to hedge diesel and jet fuels, which often trade at stable premiums to heating oil.

The trading unit for the contract is 1,000 barrels (42,000 U.S. gallons). The maximum daily price fluctuation is $0.25 per gallon ($10,500 per contract). Heating oil was trading at $1.94 per gallon as of mid-June 2006

CHAPTER 14

Natural Gas

OVERVIEW

Natural gas, a fossil fuel, has long been prized for its ability to burn cleanly and provide relatively high levels of energy. As early as 500 BCE, the Chinese started using natural gas, forcing it through bamboo pipes in order to distill drinking water from seawater. The first commercial use of natural gas was in Britain, where gas was produced from coal to light streetlamps in 1785. It was not until 1821, however, that an American, William Hart, dug the first well specifically designed to recover natural gas.

Today, natural gas represents about a quarter of total U.S. energy consumption and continues to grow in popularity because it burns so cleanly. It is colorless and odorless. Its pure form consists of a mixture of hydrocarbon gases—mainly methane, a molecule consisting of one carbon atom and four hydrogen atoms.

Scientists believe that natural gas, like other fossil fuels, was formed from the compression of organic matter deep inside the earth. Natural gas and oil are generally found together in deposits beneath the earth's crust. The deeper the deposits lie, the greater is the percentage of natural gas in the deposit relative to the amount of oil.

Normally, natural gas escapes through layers of porous rock till it reaches the earth's surface and dissipates into the air. In some locations, however, porous rock—which soaks up natural gas like a sponge—is topped by impermeable sedimentary rock, which covers the porous rock like an umbrella. Drilling through the sedimentary rock of these natural gas reservoirs releases the gas, which is under pressure, allowing it to rise to the surface and be captured by energy producers.

It is also possible to produce natural gas by utilizing tiny microorganisms, which exist in the stomachs of most animals—including humans. When the microorganisms consume organic matter, they give off methane gas, called *biogenic methane*, which can be recovered and utilized as fuel. This is the source of natural gas harvested from landfill sites, which are providing an increasing percentage of natural gas supplies.

Gas producers and distributors generally measure gas by its volume in cubic feet or by its energy capacity expressed in British thermal units (Btu). A cubic foot refers to the volume that natural gas takes up at normal temperatures. A Btu refers to the amount of natural gas required to heat one pound of water by one degree at normal pressure. There are about 1,027 Btu in one cubic foot of natural gas.

DEMAND

As with heating oil, demand for natural gas has been highly cyclical, with heaviest demand falling during the coldest months (January and February) and lowest demand during the warmest months (July and August). In recent years, however, utilities that produce the electricity that powers air conditioners during the summer have been shifting from other types of fuel to natural gas. Consequently, demand for natural gas during this time of year is rising and thereby moderating the cyclical nature of natural gas demand.

In addition to this cyclical element of demand, other elements can also play an important role. Take, for example, the weather. The colder the winter, the steeper is the spike in demand during winter months; and the hotter the summer, the steeper is the demand spike in warm months.

Pricing is also a factor in demand for natural gas. Many large consumers of gas, like utilities, have the ability to switch from gas to other fuels, such as coal. The more expensive gas prices become, the less likely such utilities are to use gas.

And the economy impacts natural gas demand as well. When the economy expands, production levels rise, forcing increases in raw material and energy purchases. During recessions, on the other hand, companies pull in their horns, with corresponding declines in production and the costs associated with production of natural gas.

Longer-term demand for natural gas will depend on residential, commercial, and industrial energy trends as well. The biggest of these drivers is expected to be future residential heating applications. In 2003, 70 percent of newly constructed single-family homes used natural gas, compared with 66 percent between 1991 and 1999, a trend that is expected to continue. The Energy Information Administration (EIA) projects residential energy demand to increase 25 percent between 2002 and 2025—1.5 percent per year from 2002 to 2010 and 0.9 percent per year from 2010 to 2025.

Likewise, the EIA anticipates increased demand for natural gas in the commercial sector, driven by cheaper prices of natural gas relative to electricity and new natural gas technologies, such as gas-powered cooling. The EIA forecasts commercial demand for natural gas to climb at an average annual rate of 1.7 percent to 2025.

In the industrial sector, the EIA anticipates increased demand for natural gas as well, but at a slower rate. According to the EIA, industrial demand for natural gas should rise at an average rate of 1.2 percent per year to 2025. This slower rate of increase is due to a movement away from energy-intensive manufacturing in the United States and a higher degree of fuel efficiency in manufacturing equipment and processes.

U.S.–delivered consumption of natural gas in 2003 fell 4.9 percent year over year to 20,192 billion cubic feet, according to preliminary figures of the *CRB Commodity Yearbook 2005*. Of this amount, 25 percent went to residences, 16 percent to commercial establishments, 24 percent to electrical utility plants, and 35 percent to industrial establishments. Analysts anticipate that total natural gas consumption will reach 31.5 trillion cubic feet by 2020.

SUPPLY

While recent demand for natural gas has been increasing in excess of 3 percent per year, supply is increasing at an annual rate of only 1 percent. In other words, shortages are plaguing not only the oil markets but the natural gas market as well.

According to 2001 data from the U.S. Energy Administration, proven U.S. natural gas reserves stand at 167 trillion cubic feet (Tcf) and represent 3.2 percent of world gas reserves. The United States consumes about 22.8 Tcf of natural gas per year and imports 3.6 Tcf, mainly from Canada

Total U.S. production of natural gas rose to 24,243 billion cubic feet in 2003, just under the record level of 24,501 billion cubic feet produced in 2001 and a 1.1 percent increase over the previous year, according to the *CRB Commodity Yearbook 2005*. Texas provided the largest share of U.S. production (26.4 percent) in 2003, followed by Oklahoma (8.3 percent), New Mexico (7.7 percent), Wyoming (7.5 percent), and Louisiana (6.9 percent).

Further increases in domestic production are anticipated, due to higher prices brought about by rising demand. Most of the new production will likely come from onshore sources, although Gulf of Mexico production is expected to grow significantly as well. Substantial expansion in Canadian imports is also expected.

To meet this country's considerable appetite for natural gas, which represented 25 percent of the worldwide consumption in 1999, the United States relies primarily on domestic production. The National Petroleum Council estimates that, based on 2002 production levels, there is enough natural gas in the United States to meet over 75 years of domestic production.

The United States also imports dry gas and liquefied natural gas (LNG). Imports of dry gas come primarily from Canada, whereas the United States gets the majority of its LNG from Trinidad and Tobago, Qatar, and Algeria.

The biggest worldwide producers of natural gas are the United States and Russia. The EIA reports that in 2002 the United States produced 23,941 billion cubic feet of natural gas, while Russia produced 21,027 billion cubic feet. Canada was the next largest producer (7,786 billion cubic feet), followed by Algeria (5,672 billion cubic feet). Imports of natural gas between countries, however, have been limited relative to other forms of energy, a situation that is expected to change. Nearly 50 percent of world oil production currently crosses a country's borders, compared with only 16 percent of the world's supply of natural gas

The U.S. natural gas market has undergone significant changes since enactment of the Natural Gas Policy Act of 1978, which helped deregulate interstate market sales of natural gas by decontrolling wellhead prices. (Regulation had been intended to protect consumers and ensure adequate supplies at fair prices; but by the mid-1970s, regulation was no longer working, and acute shortages had developed.) Following enactment of the Natural Gas Policy Act, the Federal Energy Regulatory Commission implemented rules encouraging pipelines to transport gas for third parties. Combined, these two steps stimulated new growth in oil supplies, increased competition, expanded spot market transactions, and led ultimately to the start of trading in natural gas futures.

TRADING

Deregulation of the natural gas markets has pushed price risk and competition from the producer and reseller level down to the actual retail purchasers of natural gas. In some areas of the United States, homeowners are able to lock in current gas prices through the use of long-term contracts.

Consequently, supply and demand are now the primary determinants of natural gas prices, although technical factors (e.g., pipeline capacity) as well as fundamental factors (e.g., industrial use) can impact prices as well. And the futures market has become the universally recognized mechanism for setting gas prices, which are posted instantaneously, giving both buyers and sellers a real-time look at market conditions. In other words, the futures market acts as a price reference index or benchmark for natural gas prices, ascertaining the market value of gas not just for the next delivery month but for three years into the future.

The liquidity of the futures market allows participants to lock in current prices for gas they have committed to buy or sell and to enter or exit even large positions without disrupting prices in the broader market. Without this flexibility, the only recourse for buyers and sellers trying to manage the volatility of deregulated gas prices would be to search for a counterpart with equal and opposite needs, a time-consuming exercise at best. Instead, by bringing together diverse market participants in a central forum, the futures market allows buyers and sellers to transfer their price risk to investors or commercial buyers and sellers with inverse risk profiles.

The New York Mercantile Exchange (NYMEX) Division natural gas futures contract was launched on April 3, 1990, and trades in units of 10,000 million Btu. It is based on delivery at the Henry Hub in Louisiana—a nexus of 16 intra- and interstate natural gas pipeline systems that serve markets throughout the East Coast, the Gulf Coast, and the Midwest. The contract is widely used as a national benchmark price for natural gas.

Like other futures contracts, a natural gas futures contract is a legally binding agreement between a buyer and a seller to take cash payment for a physical commodity on a specified future date for an agreed-upon price. Buyers and sellers can participate in the futures market anonymously; and a contract's quantity, delivery period, specifications and location for delivery, and timing and method of payment are standardized.

Say, for example, a marketer has agreed to sell gas in September to an electrical utility for $2 per million British thermal units (MMBtu). The marketer does not yet own the gas and so must enter the futures market to protect himself (or herself) against the risk of a price increase prior to his cash purchase of the gas. He purchases one natural gas September futures contract at a price of $2 per MMBtu.

A month later, the marketer makes the gas purchases to cover his cash market obligation, obviating the need for his protective futures contract. To terminate his futures contract, the marketer needs only to reenter the futures market and sell an offsetting contract with the same delivery month as the contract, he had earlier purchased. In so doing, he cancels his earlier contract and his obligation is terminated.

To close an open position with an offsetting contract, a contract holder must act no later than the designated last trading day for that contract. After that day, the contract holder is obligated to make delivery according to the terms of the contract. Less than 1 percent of total futures exchange volume results in actual physical delivery, however. Most are simply cancelled by the sale of offsetting contracts.

The price that the marketer in the preceding example receives for sale of an offsetting contract is unlikely to be the same price that he paid, since pricing in the volatile natural gas market can change by the minute, if not by the second. Assume that in the month since the marketer bought the September contract at $2/MMBtu spot, futures prices have risen such that the contract now sells for $2.10/MMBtu. This yields the marketer a $0.10/MMBtu ($1,000) profit on his hedge, excluding brokerage commissions. On the other hand, if prices had declined to $1.90/MMBtu, the marketer would have experienced a $0.10/MMBtu loss on his transaction, plus brokerage commissions.

The real benefit of the marketer's futures contract purchase, however, was not his $1,000 profit. Rather it was the protection that the contract afforded him. The marketer was obligated to deliver gas at a price of $2/MMBtu. By the time he was able to make his purchase in the cash market, gas prices had risen to $2.10/MMBtu, a $0.10/MMBtu ($1,000) cost increase that was offset by the sale of his futures contract.

Successful hedges such as the preceding one require a close relationship between the price of a futures contract and that of the underlying physical commodity, a relationship known as "basis"; and the closer the relationship, the better the hedge. In the example of the natural gas marketer, cash and futures prices moved in lockstep, each rising by exactly the same amount—a perfect hedge with zero basis risk.

This is seldom actually the case, however. Perfect basis relationships do not exist, and fluctuations in basis create additional risks and opportunities for hedgers. Hedgers accept this risk because the price risk they eliminate by hedging is generally greater than the basis risk that they take on. In the natural gas market, basis risk results from the possibility of deviations in two types of relationship: cash/futures basis and location basis.

Cash/futures basis alludes to the relationship between the futures price and the spot price of an underlying commodity. Any difference in these prices will disappear by termination of trading of the futures contract as a result of arbitrage—simultaneous purchases of physical commodities and sales of futures contracts (or vice versa) to profit from any discrepancies of price between the two.

Location basis plays a role when gas is bought or sold at a location other than at the futures contract delivery site. It expresses the relationship between the futures price and a spot price that gas may command at a location other than the delivery site. Normally, any differences in price should amount to the cost of transportation between the two. Until gas is able to move between the two points, however, supply-and-demand balances in each region can also affect relative prices.

Another possible use of contracts is in the implementation of spread strategies. While there are many types of spreads, they all have two things in common. First, spreads always involve at least two simultaneous futures positions. Second, price changes of the two (or more) futures positions are expected to have a reasonably predictable relationship such that changes (or anticipated changes) in this relationships would be profitable

For example, a trader might simultaneously have an obligation to buy (be long) April 10 natural gas contracts and sell (be short) June 10 natural gas contracts. The trader profits if market forces cause the price of the near-term contract to make a larger advance than the distant contract. Likewise, the trader would benefit from market forces that result in the distant contract dropping more sharply than the near-term contract. This type of spread—where all of the futures positions are in the same type of commodity—is called an *intramarket* spread.

Spreads are also possible using two different types of commodities that display a price relationship, such as natural gas and propane. These types of spreads are called *intermarket* spreads.[*]

---

[*]Adapted from *Risk Management with Natural Gas Futures and Options* (New York Mercantile Exchange, Inc., 1998).

PART FIVE

Speculating in Tropical Commodities

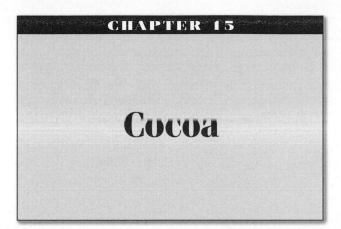

CHAPTER 15

Cocoa

OVERVIEW

Cocoa's origins are thought to have been in the Amazon basin, from where it spread to Central America and Mexico. The Maya considered cocoa to be food of the gods; Aztecs used cocoa seeds as currency. Christopher Columbus was the first European to discover cocoa beans in the late 15th century. The beans did not become popular in Europe until some 20 years later, however, when Hernando Cortes sent cocoa beans, along with Aztec cocoa recipes, back to Charles V, the king of Spain. Hot cocoa became popular with the Spanish aristocracy, who planted beans in Spain's overseas possessions, thereby establishing a thriving industry.

By 1828, a cocoa press had been developed that allowed for the development of a new cocoa product—cocoa butter. Later in the 19th century, around 1879, the Swiss developed the cocoa products that have become for many a favorite treat: solid chocolate and milk chocolate. Today the chocolate market is the biggest consumer of cocoa beans, accounting for about two-thirds of world bean production, while cocoa butter, used in the manufacture of tobacco, soap, and cosmetics, uses roughly one-third of world production. Cocoa cake, cocoa liquor, and cocoa powder also utilize some market share.

Cocoa is a mild stimulant due to the presence of an alkaloid (theobromine) that is closely related to caffeine. Its food value is high, containing as much as 20 percent protein, 40 percent carbohydrate, and 40 percent fat.

Cocoa grows on trees in hot, rainy climates; and cultivation of the plant is concentrated in a narrow band that extends 20 degrees north and south of the equator. To thrive, cocoa trees need 1,150 to 2,500 millimeters of rain annually and temperatures that range between 21 and 32 degrees centigrade.

The leading producers of cocoa beans currently are the Ivory Coast (40.6 percent of world production in 2004 to 2005), Ghana (19 percent), and Indonesia (13 percent). But while cocoa is primarily produced in developing countries, it is mostly consumed in Europe, North America, Japan, and Singapore. Ghana and Indonesia have been seeking to increase their share of cocoa production; but Ghana must also cope with two ongoing problems: black pod disease and the smuggling of its crop across the border into Ivory Coast.

Sharp price changes often occur, depending on the numerous developments that influence the market price of cocoa beans. Changing crop prospects, caused by unexpected drought or other adverse weather while the crop is growing, and damage by insects and cocoa tree diseases make it difficult to foretell the exact amount of future supplies. Sometimes, manmade barriers, such as wars, strikes, or political developments in the tropical producing areas, retard the movement of supplies to the United States and other consuming nations.

Volatility also occurs due to the rigors of changing conditions, such as trends in the business cycle that influence buying power in the consuming countries. Sometimes, high cocoa prices reduce the rate of actual consumption, while low prices may stimulate demand. Other factors that impact pricing include consolidation within the cocoa industry, changing inventory practices, and privatization of production companies in key West African nations. And the concentration of cocoa growers in Ghana and the Ivory Coast, which together account for 55 percent of worldwide production of cocoa beans, means that political and social issues in these countries can have tremendous impact on the cocoa market.

DEMAND

Consumption of cocoa is generally measured by the amount of cocoa ground for use, known as the *quarterly cocoa grind*. The quarterly grind figures can be easily accessed through the New York Board of Trade (NYBOT) web site.

World consumption of cocoa rose 7.2 percent to a record high of 3.219 million metric tons in 2003 to 2004, according to the *CRB Commodity Yearbook 2005*. The combined countries of the European Union were the world's biggest consumers (36 percent of world consumption) followed by the United States (13 percent). And within the European Union, data from the International Cocoa Organization indicate that the biggest consumers were Germany (9.1 percent of world consumption), France (7.2 percent), and the United Kingdom (6.8 percent).

The United States is the primary destination of beans exported from Latin America, while most of Africa's beans go to Europe. Asian imports come mainly from Indonesia, Malaysia, and South American countries.

A few multinational companies in the cocoa-consuming countries dominate the processing of cocoa beans and the manufacture of chocolate products. The Netherlands has historically been the leading processor of cocoa, providing approximately 15 percent of the world's annual production of cocoa; but in recent years, the United States has become a close competitor in bean processing. In 2004, the United States imported a record high 1.171 million metric tons of cocoa and cocoa products—an 11.9 percent increase over the previous year and 64 percent more than the United States imported in 1990.

SUPPLY

Most cocoa production takes place on small farms in the primary growing countries, although some large plantations do exist, primarily in Brazil, Ecuador, and Malaysia.

Cocoa trees take 4 or 5 years after planting to yield cocoa beans and from 8 to 10 years to achieve maximum production; but they can live for 50 years or more. During its growing season, a cocoa tree will produce thousands of flowers; but only a few flowers develop cocoa pods.

Where ideal conditions exist (a consistent balance of rainy season and plenty of sun), harvesting can be essentially continuous, occurring almost every month. Countries with more distinctly separate dry and wet seasons normally harvest twice a year (a main crop and a mid-crop). Total annual world production in recent years has been around the 3 million metric ton mark.

There are three varieties of cocoa trees. The most common, *Forastero*, accounts for 90 percent of the world's supply of cocoa beans. It grows primarily in West Africa and Brazil. A second type of tree, *Criollo*, produces beans much desired for their flavor and are found in parts of the Caribbean, Venezuela, Papua New Guinea, the West Indies, Sri Lanka, East Timor, and Java. The third variety, *Trinitario*, is a cross from Forastero and Criollo.

Successful cocoa production depends heavily on the availability of land within a tropical rain forest, the ideal growing environment for cocoa trees. It also depends on access to labor to help harvest the cocoa, a process that does not lend itself to mechanization.

When cocoa pods are ripe, workers must cut down the pods, open them, and remove the seeds. The seeds are then fermented and dried by air and sun. A single pod generally yields 20 to 30 beans, and about 400 beans are required to make one pound of chocolate.

Disease and weather can seriously impair harvest productivity. Black pod, for example, has become a major threat to African bean production. Brazil's growers suffered an epidemic of witch's broom virus in the 1990s, which badly damaged Brazil's bean production.

From 2004 to 2005, world cocoa production tumbled 8.6 percent to 3.13 million metric tons, compared with a record-high 3.423 million metric tons the previous year according to the *CRB Commodity Yearbook 2005*. The decline was due largely to shortfalls in Ivory Coast production levels. In November 2004, fighting broke out between the Ivory Coast government, rebel groups, and France, which led to a temporary 25 percent drop in cocoa production and shipments from the Ivory Coast. This resulted in a 2004–2005 decline of 8.4 percent from record previous-year Ivory Coast production levels of 1.386 million metric tons.

TRADING

The fact that cocoa is primarily produced in developing countries and largely consumed in North America, Europe, and Japan has posed substantial challenges for the production process. Most cocoa is harvested between October and January; and for proper storage, it is necessary to move the cocoa from the tropics to temperate zones quickly. Historically, this forced intermediary merchants to assume considerable financial risk by carrying harvested cocoa until processors were ready for it. The solution would have been a futures market to hedge bean prices over the interim period, but it took a market disaster to spur the industry into establishing an organized cocoa exchange.

That disaster came in the form of a commodity boom and bust in the wake of World War I when cocoa was a favorite speculative commodity. Speculators loaded up on cocoa beans and stored them in an effort to push prices higher. Manufacturers were forced to compete with these speculators to fill their required orders, which led to unstable price hikes. In 1921, when speculators unloaded inventories to repay past-due bank loans, the market crashed, taking with it the fortunes of many participants in the cocoa market. This led the cocoa industry to finally establish a cocoa futures exchange in 1925.

Cocoa futures now trade on the NYBOT's Coffee, Sugar, and Cocoa Exchange (CSCE) Division and the London International Financial Futures and Options Exchange (LIFFE). The contracts call for delivery of 10 metric tons (22,046 pounds) of cocoa and are priced in U.S. dollars per metric ton. And the minimum price fluctuation of cocoa futures is one dollar per metric ton.

The NYBOT lists contracts for trading more than 18 months out, which accommodates the long-term cycle of the cocoa production process (a surplus or shortage of cocoa can lead to sharp price fluctuations long before the cash market can adjust the supply of cocoa). As with other commodities, cocoa futures are usually closed out before delivery can take place.

A hedger in the futures market is a cocoa merchant who must acquire the bulk of his or her supply when cocoa is harvested in the fall and early winter. The merchant must then carry that inventory until processors need it. The risk that the merchant faces is the possibility of severe losses if the price of cocoa declines significantly during this holding period.

To hedge this risk, the merchant—when he (or she) makes his cocoa acquisition from the producing country—can immediately sell on the futures exchange an amount of cocoa futures equivalent to the bean supply purchased. Then, when the merchant sells the actual cocoa, he simultaneously buys back cocoa futures in an amount equivalent to the futures he previously sold as a hedge, thereby canceling the hedge.

If the price of cocoa has declined, the merchant will make up for any loss on his inventory sale with a profit from buying back the futures contract at a lower price. Likewise, if bean prices rise and the merchant incurs a loss from buying back the futures contracts at a higher price, this loss will be offset by a gain in the sale of his actual inventory.

Chocolate manufacturers can likewise mitigate risk by utilizing the futures market. The NYBOT provides the example of a chocolate manufacturer who has contracted to sell a quantity of chocolate at a fixed price for delivery in August/September. His projected selling price (and profit margin) for the chocolate is based on a current cocoa bean futures price of $1,263 per metric ton.

To produce the chocolate, the chocolate manufacturer will need 50 metric tons of cocoa beans, which he has not yet purchased. This poses a dilemma for the chocolate maker. He is unwilling to tie up the capitol necessary to buy and store the beans until he needs them, yet he fears that there could be a significant price increase in the beans before he contracts to buy them.

The NYBOT suggests the following strategy.[*]

---

[*]Reprinted by permission of the New York Board of Trade® (NYBOT®), New York's original futures exchange and the global marketplace for "soft" commodities.

To manage this price risk, the manufacturer buys 5 July 2002 contracts (50 metric tons ÷ 10 tons per contract = 5 contracts). The July contract best approximates the time he expects to purchase the beans in the cash market. With the futures transaction, the manufacturer has locked in a buy price (1263) that protects his profit margin in the sale of his chocolate.

1/3/02—buy 5 July 2002 futures at 1263

Result: *In early July, cocoa prices have risen, and the manufacturer purchases the needed beans in the cash market and simultaneously unwinds his futures hedge by selling the position back to the market:*

7/2/02—sell 5 July 2002 futures at 1682

The manufacturer's futures hedge strategy has generated a futures profit of $20,950:

5 contracts × [(Sell price less buy price) × $10 Tick value]

or

$$5 \times [(1682 - 1263) \times \$10] = \$20,950$$

While the manufacturer's cash purchase price for the cocoa is higher in July than it would have been in January, the $20,950 profit from the hedge will offset some or all of the higher cash price, thus achieving the manufacturer's goal of managing price risk by locking in an acceptable purchase price for the cocoa beans (1263) and protecting profit margins. Had the price of cocoa fallen, the corresponding futures loss would be offset by the increased cash market gain. The result would be the same, namely, protecting a profit margin based on a specific purchase price (1263).

Such hedging is absolutely essential for the business survival of companies in the cocoa industry. The NYBOT reports that the magnitude of cocoa price changes is often greater than the size of average profit margins all along the marketing chain. For example, the NYBOT notes that between December of 2001 and April of 2002, the price of the nearby cocoa futures contract jumped more than 50 percent.

Typical hedgers in the cocoa market include candy manufacturers, cocoa importers and exporters, and cocoa producers. All face significant risk from the volatility of cocoa prices, risk that futures speculators are willing to assume in exchange for profit opportunities.

All trading in the NYBOT cocoa futures market, whether by hedgers or speculators, requires a fundamental knowledge of the underlying cash market as well as an understanding of the function of futures markets. As with any futures market, traders should be familiar with the tools of technical analysis and follow a clear trading plan that identifies both goals and risk tolerance levels.

CHAPTER 16

Coffee

OVERVIEW

The word *coffee* comes from Kaffa, the region in Ethiopia where coffee originated. From Ethiopia, coffee seedlings spread throughout Arabia and Turkey. It was not until 1683, however, that coffee made its way to Europe. Invading Turkish armies were stopped outside Vienna, leaving behind sacks of coffee beans. Coffee consumption quickly spread and not only became a staple of European diets but also played a central role in European trade and commerce.

The French first brought coffee to the Americas, planting trees in Martinique and Brazil, while the Jesuits are credited with bringing coffee to Columbia. Europeans also brought coffee with them to the American colonies, where coffee soon replaced tea as the most popular beverage. Today, over 500 billion cups of coffee are served worldwide every year, and U.S. coffee drinkers alone consume three and one-half cups per day.

Coffee beans grow on a tropical evergreen shrub that can grow up to 100 feet tall. The tree grows best in tropical areas between the Tropics of Cancer and Capricorn. It requires year-round warm temperatures averaging about 70 degrees Fahrenheit and abundant rainfall.

A new coffee tree takes from three to five years to yield a pound of coffee. If the tree survives disease, insects, drought, flooding, earthquakes, and frost, it can have a lifespan of 20 to 25 years. Each year a typical fully groomed tree will yield enough beans (about 4,000 beans) to fill a one-pound can of ground coffee on the supermarket shelf. Coffee is generally produced on small land holdings. Coffee is grown in more than 50 countries along the earth's warmer latitudes at altitudes from sea level to 6,000 feet.

Coffee cultivation begins with nurturing the seedlings for 9 to 18 months in nurseries or in sun-sheltered clusters. When the seedlings grow to about 24 inches, they are transplanted to permanent groves but are still protected from overexposure to sun. It takes another 18 months to achieve flowering. Six months later, green berries begin to bud and ripen into rich red "cherries." Inside each cherry, within a reddish-yellow pulp and sheathed in a silvery, parchment-like jacket, are two coffee beans ready for harvesting. The beans are removed from the cherries by one of two methods: washed or unwashed.

The beans are then bagged for transportation to the warehouse for export. Overall, export coffee income of the producing regions has averaged about $14 billion a year. The United States is the largest importer of coffee.

The aroma and flavor of coffee are still locked within the green beans when they arrive at the points of entry. The beans are shipped to roasting houses, where they are roasted to golden brown and swell to about twice their original size. After roasting, the beans are left to cool to room temperature and are then shuttled into machines that granulate the beans into grinds best suited for the different types of coffeemakers. The grinds are packaged in vacuum-tight cans or in sealed bags for distribution to the supermarkets or grocery stores. In addition to these traditional retailers, there are purveyors such as Starbucks that also sell beans whole or ground.

Instant coffee is made from roasted coffee and steamed into a beverage, which is then dehydrated, leaving tiny crystals of strong brewed coffee. When boiling water is added, the crystals dissolve and create the beverage. Freeze-dried coffee is a variation of instant; since it utilizes a more expensive technology, it costs more than regular instant. With freeze-dried coffee, the strong brewed coffee is frozen at extremely low temperatures and then dried in a vacuum to preserve more freshness of the original brew. Steaming the green beans until soft and removing the caffeine from the beans, which are then processed in the conventional manner, makes decaffeinated coffee.

For decades, the countries dependent on coffee exports for the revenue essential to their development suffered from the destabilizing effects of boom-and-bust cycles. The booms were short, but each triggered a new round of overproduction, which in turn led to long periods of bust because the excess coffee stocks depressed export prices.

In 1962, the governments of the major exporting and importing countries negotiated the first International Coffee Agreement in a joint attempt to prevent extreme price fluctuations in the world market. The agreement of 1962 lasted for five years and was followed by the agreements of 1968 and 1976. President Kennedy was a prime mover for the first coffee agreement. He voiced his belief that the persisting decline in coffee prices was undermining his Alliance for Progress program to assist the development of Latin America. Every succeeding president has also supported ideas leading to the coffee agreements.

DEMAND

It is estimated that more than 500 billion cups of coffee are served worldwide each year. The U.S. Department of Agriculture (USDA) estimates that worldwide consumption of coffee rose 2 percent to 119.9 million bags in 2004 to 2005. That was slightly higher than the 1.5 percent average growth rate in recent years. Europe is the world leader in coffee consumption (46.428 million bags in 2003), followed by the United States.

U.S. coffee consumption climbed 7 percent to 22 million bags in 2004 (*CRB Commodity Yearbook 2005*) compared with 20.505 million bags in 2003. The National Coffee Association (NCA) reported in 2000 that 54 percent of adult Americans drink coffee daily, and it projected that each coffee drinker spends an average of $164.71 on coffee annually.

Based on USDA data, European consumption is led by Germany (9.133 million bags in 2003), Italy (5.503 million bags in 2003) and France (5.428 million bags in 2003). Japan, also a major importer of coffee beans, consumed 6.770 million bags in 2003 (USDA).

The world's largest exporters of coffee are Brazil (30 percent of world exports in 2004 to 2005/USDA), Vietnam (15 percent/USDA), and Columbia (11 percent/USDA). The biggest imports into the United States in 2004 came from Brazil (20 percent of U.S. imports *CRB Commodity Yearbook 2005*), Columbia (17 percent *CRB Commodity Yearbook 2005*), Mexico (7 percent), and Guatemala (7 percent *CRB Commodity Yearbook 2005*).

SUPPLY

There are two types of coffee: *Arabica*, the most widely used, represents 70 percent of all coffee produced. It grows in high altitudes—600 to 2,000 meters—primarily in Columbia and Brazil. *Robusta* is a hardier and cheaper type of coffee to grow, but its taste is considered to be inferior to Arabica. Robusta grows at lower altitudes, mainly in Indonesia, West Africa, Brazil, and Vietnam.

Major commodity trading houses, such as Nestle, Procter & Gamble, and Sara Lee, as well as domestic retailers such as Starbucks, dominate the world's coffee markets. These companies represent 60 percent of coffee sales in the United States and 40 percent of global coffee trade.

While seasonal changes impact coffee prices, there is no seasonal peak in coffee production. Freeze scares in Brazil can boost prices in the summer months (Brazil experiences a major freeze about every five years). And demand generally declines by about 12 percent from the year's average during the summer months.

The USDA forecast 2005–2006 world coffee production of 113.2 million bags (December 2005), a decline of 7 percent from 2004 to 2005, due partially to rain damage from hurricanes. There was also damage to the coffee infrastructure in 2005 due to hurricanes, especially in Mexico.

The USDA forecast 2005–2006 total coffee supply in producing countries of 139.2 million bags (December 2005), down 4 percent from 2004–2005 levels. All the decrease is the result of lower production.

TRADING

Historically, the degree of volatility in coffee prices has been significantly greater than for other commodities, such as cocoa or sugar. Most producing countries (e.g., Brazil, Colombia, El Salvador, Nicaragua, Panama, Ethiopia, and Zaire) need foreign exchange to pay for oil imports. Consequently, they tend to export coffee as quickly as they can, which inevitably leads to surpluses and serves as a price depressant. Also contributing to price volatility is the price sensitivity of coffee users. If coffee approaches $4 per pound, consumption falls off sharply. Finally, coffee production's vulnerability to weather stresses as well as its limitations of climate and geography further ensures constant volatility of coffee prices.

Coffee futures and options markets cannot remove the volatility in coffee prices, but they do allow coffee industry participants to transfer and manage this risk. By the same token, futures markets provide speculators with the opportunity to profit from coffee's price volatility. The numerous variables that can impact coffee's price, however, require speculators in futures contracts to exercise great care in devising his or her trading strategy, whether "long," "short," or "spread."

Arabica coffee trades on the Coffee, Sugar, and Cocoa Exchange (CSCE) Division of the New York Board of Trade (NYBOT). Robusta trades on the London International Financial Futures and Options Exchange (LIFFE). Coffee futures also trade on the Bolsa de Mercadorias & Futuros (BM&F) in Rio de Janeiro and the Tokyo Grain Exchange (TGE).

The NYBOT coffee market trades the Coffee "C"® Futures Contract and the Mini Coffee "C" Futures Contract. Each Coffee "C" futures contract (ticker symbol KC) traded in the NYBOT coffee market is for 37,500 pounds (approximately 250 bags) of Exchange-certified Arabica coffee. The contract has a minimum price fluctuation of .05 cents/pound equivalent to $18.75 per contract. At 70 cents/pound, one contract would be worth $26,250.

The Mini "C" Contract (equivalent to 12,500 pounds of Arabica coffee) is designed to provide access to the NYBOT market for smaller producers, retailers, and investors for whom the regular "C" contract is impractical. The Mini "C" contract has many of the same specifications as the regular. It differs primarily in size and settlement provisions. At one-third the size of the regular, the Mini "C" (12,500 pounds) is cash settled. Assuming a price of 70 cents/pound, for example, the contract would have a total value $8,750 and a minimum price fluctuation equivalent to $6.25 per contract.

The NYBOT Coffee "C" contract is now generally used by the coffee industry to price Arabica coffees. And the Coffee "C" regular futures contract nearest to expiration is used as a benchmark for cash pricing.

Basis—the difference between the New York spot futures price and the cash price at the local delivery point—is an important factor in pricing and hedging coffee. For example, coffee delivered at the Port of New Orleans trades at a discount to coffee delivered in New York. Basis is not constant—it changes over time and provides both risks and opportunities.

As an essential element in cash pricing, the grading of coffee contributes to the basis differential. The coffee industry prices coffee based on consistent standards of quality. The Specialty Coffee Association of America (SCAA), for example, divides green coffee into five defined grades based on the number of full defects (e.g., imperfections such as stones, sticks, and spoiled or broken beans) found in formal sampling of the coffee.

The Class 3, or exchange grade of Arabica coffee in the SCAA classification, is comparable to the standard benchmark for pricing coffee. All other coffees trade at a premium or a discount to the Arabica standard for the Coffee "C" contract. A premium grade of coffee (Class 2), for example, might trade at 25 cents/pound above the nearby coffee futures price. The differential is negotiated in the cash market but uses the nearby Coffee "C" futures contract as a base price.

Many segments of the coffee industry hedge with Coffee "C" futures, including producers, importers, exporters, trade houses, and roasters. While these hedgers may pursue different futures strategies, their goal is the same: to protect their bottom line, which would otherwise be exposed to adverse price moves.

While the most common methods of hedging utilize futures, strategies can evolve into options or futures/options combinations as well as simultaneous cash and futures transactions and Exchange for Swaps Transactions (EFS). The NYBOT offers the following example of futures hedging.[*]

Scenario: On March 5, a coffee roaster is committed to receive a delivery of 300,000 pounds of green coffee on or about June 4. The roaster has tried and failed to obtain a price-to-be-fixed contract with the dealer. The Coffee "C"® nearby contract price on the scheduled delivery day will be the benchmark to determine the cash price for the shipment. The roaster's delivery price is therefore unknown.

July futures are trading at 59.45 cents/lb. on March 5. The roaster's assessment of the market historical patterns and current conditions suggests that prices are likely to rise in the next three months. The roaster, therefore, is exposed to a price risk.

July Futures @ 59.45 cents/lb.

Strategy: Since the roaster's cash market delivery is scheduled for June 3, the cash market delivery price is pegged to the then nearby (July) contract. Therefore, the roaster would need eight July contracts (each contract is for 37,500 lbs./250 bags) to cover his entire green coffee delivery of 300,000 lbs./2,000 bags. The roaster decides the July futures price is one that will result in a reasonable profit for his operation, so he buys eight July futures contracts at 59.45 cents/lb.

37,500 lbs. × 8 contracts = 300,000 lbs.

8 July Futures @ 59.45 cents/lb.

Result: On June 4, July coffee futures are trading at 72.70 cents/lb. The roaster pays 68.70 for his cash market delivery and immediately places an order with his broker, who sends the order to the exchange floor to close out (sell) his eight futures contracts at (or near) that price. In the cash market, the roaster has paid 9.25 cents/lb. more than expected; but the 9.25 cents/lb. gain in the futures market gives the roaster a net price of 59.45, the target price back in March.

---

[*]Reprinted by permission of the New York Board of Trade® (NYBOT®), New York's original futures exchange and the global marketplace for "soft" commodities.

74.70 cents/lb. (June 4 futures price) – 59.45 (March 5 futures price)
= 15.25 cents/lb. (futures gain)

74.70 (cash price) – 15.25 (futures gain) = 59.45 (target price)

If the price had fallen during that same period, the roaster would still achieve a target price of 59.45 with the gain in the cash market balanced against the loss in the futures market. Achieving the target price is the key objective of futures hedging. By locking in the June price back in March, the roaster had protected his profit margin.

CHAPTER 17

Sugar

OVERVIEW

Sugars, which are known for their sweet taste, are the simplest molecules that can be identified as a carbohydrate and come in multiple forms, including sucrose, dextrose, fructose, and lactose. The form of sugar most commonly found in processed foods—sucrose—is made from one molecule of glucose and one molecule of fructose. The two primary sources of sucrose are sugarcane and sugar beets.

Sugarcane is a tropical grass that is thought to have originated in New Guinea and spread throughout the Pacific Islands to India. The first known process for extracting sugar from sugarcane was developed in India about 500 BCE and consisted of pressing out the sugarcane's juice and boiling it into crystals.

With the Persian invasion of India by Emperor Darius in 510 BCE, use of sugarcane spread across Persia. But it was only with the Arab invasions of Persia in 642 CE that the secret of sugarcane production penetrated beyond Persia to Spain, North Africa, and—with the onset of the Crusades in the 11th century—Europe.

Initially, Europeans were dependent on imports from tropical regions of Asia and the Middle East for their sugar, which was a luxury item costing the equivalent of $100 per kilo. Then in 1493, Columbus carried cuttings of sugarcane with him to the West Indies, where cane thrived. And a little over a century later, the Portuguese introduced sugar production to Brazil. In 1625 the Dutch carried sugarcane from South America to the Caribbean

Islands. These colonies became thriving new sources for sugarcane, which grew on large plantations supported by slave labor imported from Africa.

Sugarcane continued to dominate European consumption until 1813, when Napoleon, cut off from Caribbean imports of sugar by a British blockade, banned sugar imports. Instead, Europe turned to sugar beets, whose roots had been identified as a source of sugar in 1747 by a German chemist. By 1880, sugar beets, which are annuals that grow in temperate or colder climates, had replaced sugarcane as the dominant source of sugar in continental Europe.

Sugar beets were introduced into Britain some 150 years later when World War I threatened Britain's sugar imports. And sugar beet production in the United States was largely initiated by Mormons, who began raising sugar beets in Utah during the second half of the 19th century. By the early 1900s, beet production had become profitable in the United States, and many new beet sugar factories were established in the West.

Sugarcane, a perennial member of the grass family, grows best in hot wet climates where heavy rainfalls are followed by a dry season. It is found in tropical and subtropical regions of the world that lie between the Tropics of Cancer and Capricorn. The major sugarcane producing countries are Brazil, India, China, and Thailand in that order. In the United States, the leading producer states are Florida, Louisiana, Texas, and Hawaii.

The sugar beet, an annual, grows from seeds and does best in areas with moderate temperatures and evenly distributed rainfall. Sugar is stored in the root of the sugar beet, which is planted in the spring and harvested in the fall before the onset of heavy frosts. The biggest producers of sugar beets worldwide are Europe, the United States, China, and Japan. In the United States, the leading producers are Minnesota, Idaho, North Dakota, and Michigan.

Sugar beets account for about 25 percent of all the sugar produced in the world, with the remainder coming from sugarcane. Current trends show the overall production of sugar from sugarcane is increasing relative to that produced from sugar beets. There is no distinction in taste between sugar from cane and sugar from beet roots; but because beets must be planted from seed each year, their production costs are higher than those associated with sugarcane.

Between 1990 and 2002, the cost of producing refined sugar dropped almost 13 percent, while consumer prices rose. For example, cereal prices climbed 20 percent, candy prices increased 22 percent, and prices for cookies and cakes rose 30 percent. Sugar is among the most heavily subsidized agricultural products. The European Union, the United States, and Japan maintain elevated price floors for sugar by subsidizing domestic production and assessing high tariffs on imports. Sugar prices in these countries have been three times the price on the international market.

Unlike coffee, where quality standards depend on the original beans, standards for sugar depend on the sugar's milling and refinement. These processes remove unwanted components like color and ash and increase sugar's sucrose level.

DEMAND

About 70 percent of worldwide sugar production is currently consumed in its country of origin. The remaining 30 percent is traded on world markets, where sugar prices are one of the most volatile of all commodity prices. ⁊

Global sugar consumption has increased by about 2.4 percent per year over the past decade, a slight increase over the long-term annual average of 2 percent. Illovo Group projections of top sugar consumers on a per capita basis in 2004–2005 included Brazil (about 54 kilograms), Mexico (52 kilograms), Australia (46 kilograms), and the European Union (39 kilograms). About 80 percent of world import demand for sugar is now from developing countries.

Domestic consumption of raw sugar worldwide rose 0.6 percent year over year to 139.311 million metric tons in 2004–2005. The U.S. Department of Agriculture (USDA) forecasts that 2005–2006 worldwide consumption will climb at a slightly faster rate of 1 percent year over year, for a total of 140.456 million metric tons.

U.S. domestic consumption of sugar grew at over twice the worldwide rate in 2004–2005—1.4 percent year over year, for a total of 9.815 million short tons (USDA). The USDA projects U.S. sugar consumption of 10.365 million short tons in 2005–2006.

From a historical perspective, however, U.S. consumption of sugar has been declining. Current U.S. per capita consumption of 29 kilograms is approximately two-thirds of U.S. sugar-consumption levels in the early 1970s. Cutting into U.S. sugar demand has been competition from glucose syrups—cheap sugar substitutes that are made from wheat and corn. The USDA notes that by 2000, corn sweeteners represented 55 percent of sweeteners used in the United States, compared with only 16 percent in 1970.

Health concerns about the relationship between sugar consumption and the alarming increase in Americans affected by obesity and diabetes are also impacting demand for sugar. A 2003 report commissioned by four United Nations agencies stated that sugar should account for no more than 10 percent of a healthy diet.

SUPPLY

The world's largest producer of sugar in 2004–2005 was Brazil (28.175 million metric tons/USDA), accounting for 19 percent of world production. Brazil was also the largest exporter (18.02 million metric tons/USDA). The next-largest producer, accounting for 12 percent of the world's 2004–2005 sugar production, was the European Union (21.825 million metric tons/USDA), which exported only 5.382 million metric tons in 2004–2005 (USDA). India, the third-largest sugar producer, generated 14.21 million metric tons in 2004–2005, a 6 percent decline from the previous year. The USDA forecasts production of 18.42 million metric tons of sugar for India in 2005–2006.

Total worldwide sugar production equaled 140.811 million metric tons in 2004–2005, according to the USDA, a 4.8 percent drop from 142.4 million metric tons in 2003–2004. The USDA projects a slight rise in world production to 144.151 million metric tons in 2005–2006.

As the sugar market has become less regulated, sugar has changed from a bulk commodity that is produced in many countries to a commodity whose production is concentrated in a few countries. Brazil, Australia, Thailand, the European Union, and Cuba currently account for about 72 percent of world free market exports of sugar, compared with 65 percent in 1985.

TRADING

Deregulation has increased some of the risks of participating in sugar markets, including price risk, currency risk, and counterparty risk in the form of new private sector participants who add to counterparty performance uncertainty. Futures exchanges remove counterparty uncertainty from exchange transactions, thereby ensuring the integrity of the contracts sold on a given exchange.

Currency fluctuations, such as sudden devaluations of emerging market currencies relative to the U.S. dollar, can impact sugar prices because prices are dollar denominated. In fact, there is a higher correlation between sugar prices and the value of the U.S. dollar than there is for many other commodities.

There are generally two components to the price of world sugar: the price of the related futures contract and the premium or discount (i.e., the basis) of the sugar to the futures contract. The price of a sugar futures contract and the basis tend to have a negative correlation—when one moves up the other moves down. For importers and exporters of sugar, freight costs are another element of sugar pricing and can account for 10 percent to 20 ✓ percent of sugar's total price.

Hedgers who use futures contracts to hedge against significant shifts in the price of sugar include producers, exporters, candy manufacturers, trade houses, bakers, refiners, and dealers. The heaviest speculators are generally managed commodity funds and arbitrageurs.✓

Sugar futures are traded on a number of world exchanges, including the Bolsa de Mercadorias & Futures (BM&F), the Kansai Commodities Exchange (KANEX), the Tokyo Grain Exchange (TGE), the London International Financial Futures and Options Exchange (LIFFE), and the CSCE Division of the New York Board of Trade (NYBOT).

The CSCE Division of the NYBOT trades raw sugar, while the LIFFE trades white sugar. The most actively traded sugar contract is the NYBOT's No. 11 (World) sugar contract, which calls for delivery of 112,000 pounds (50 long tons) of raw cane centrifugal sugar from any of 28 foreign countries of origin and the United States. The NYBOT also trades the No. 14 sugar contract, which requires delivery of 112,000 pounds of raw centrifugal cane sugar at specified Atlantic Gulf ports. Contracts for white sugar on the LIFFE call for delivery of 50 metric tons of white beet sugar, cane crystal sugar, or refined sugar of any origin from the crop current at the time of delivery.

The size of the NYBOT No. 11 sugar contract gives the contract a relatively small underlying value per contract. For example, one contract would be worth $7,840 if sugar were selling at $0.07 per pound (112,000 times $0.07). This smaller price makes the No. 11 contract attractive for speculators but also provides easier market access for smaller hedgers.

The following example offered by the NYBOT illustrates how a hedger can lock in a specific price for sugar. The hedger must maintain a margin account for as long as the position remains open and may be required to make payments to the margin account to maintain the required margin level, which ultimately could require payment in full of the contract's underlying value.[*]

Scenario: In August, a sugar refiner expects sugar prices to increase by late winter. The refiner must take delivery of 224,000 lbs. of raw sugar in February. The cash price will be benchmarked to the March Sugar No. 11^{SM} futures price. March futures are trading at 8.00 cents/lb. In order to protect his profit margin, he needs to keep his cash market price from going any higher than 8.00 cents/lb.

---

[*]Reprinted by permission of the New York Board of Trade® (NYBOT®), New York's original futures exchange and the global marketplace for "soft" commodities.

March Sugar No. 11 futures @ 8.00 cents/lb. (in August)

Strategy: *The refiner buys 2 March Sugar No. 11 Futures contracts at 8.00 cents/lb. Each contract covers 112,000 lbs. of sugar.*

Buy 2 March Sugar No. 11 Futures @ 8.00 cents/lb.

Result (rising market): *In February, sugar prices have risen as expected. March futures are trading at 9.80 cents/lb. The refiner closes out the futures position (sells 2 March Futures) @ 9.80 cents/lb., leaving the refiner with a futures market gain of 1.80 cents/lb.*

9.80 cents/lb (Feb. price) – 8.00 cents/lb (August price)
= 1.80 cents/lb. futures gain

The 1.80 cents/lb. futures gain is then used to offset the cash market shortfall when the refiner has to pay 9.80 cents/lb. for the 224,000 lbs. of raw sugar. By offsetting the cash market loss with the futures gain, the refiner has paid a net price of 8.00 cents/lb. for the raw sugar, thereby achieving his price goal (8.00 cents/lb.) and protecting the profit margin.

9.80 cents/lb. (cash price) – 1.80 cents/lb. (futures gain)
= 8.00 cents/lb. (net buy price)

Result (falling market): *If the price had fallen below 8.00 cents/lb. to 7.25 cents/lb., the refiner's futures market loss of 0.75 cents/lb. would be offset by the more favorable cash price paid (7.25 cents/lb.). The result would still yield the same net buy price of 8.00 cents/lb. It is important to remember the goal in futures hedging: Lock in an acceptable price that will achieve business goals and protect profit margins.*

7.25 cents/lb. (cash market price) + 0.75 cents/lb.
(futures market loss) = 8.00 cents/lb. (net buy price)

CHAPTER 18

Cotton

OVERVIEW

The oldest use of cotton currently known was in the Americas. Pieces of cotton cloth and bits of cotton bolls found in caves in Mexico suggest that the use of cotton dates back at least 7,000 years. By 3,000 BCE, people in the Indus River Valley of Pakistan were raising and weaving cotton into cloth. Egyptians made and used cotton cloth during this period as well.

Cotton came to Europe around 800 CE with Arab merchants and by 1500 was known and used throughout most of the world. It is thought that cotton was first planted in the United States in Florida in 1556 and in Virginia in 1607. While colonists continued to grow cotton in the United States, it was not until the invention of the cotton gin in 1703 and, in England, the spinning machine in 1730 that cotton growing became an international industry.

Some three centuries later, cotton has become the leading cash crop for the United States and the most-used fiber in the world. In the United States alone, annual revenue from cotton exceeds $120 billion.

No part of the cotton plant is left unused. The seeds are crushed for oil, which is used in cooking and food production. The leftover meal and hulls from the plant are used as fertilizer and in animal and fish food. And cotton growers plow the plant's stalk and leaves back into the ground to enrich the soil.

Like sugar and other tropical commodities, cotton grows in warm climates, primarily in the southern United States, Uzbekistan, China, and
India. The cotton belt of the United States stretches from Florida to North
Carolina and extends from the Atlantic to the Pacific. The leading producers of cotton in the United States during 2005 were Texas, Arkansas, Mis-
sissippi, Georgia, California, and North Carolina.

Planting times vary from late winter in the south to early summer in the
north—the cotton growth cycle requires about 200 frost-free days. Cotton
blooms 8 to 11 weeks after planting, with blossoms changing from white to
dark red before withering and leaving green pods called cotton bolls. Machines then pull the bolls from mature cotton plants and pack them into
bales for shipping to cotton mills.

In the past half-century, advances in weed and pest control, improved
plant varieties and fertilizers, as well as refinements in agricultural equipment have vastly increased the productivity of the United States cotton industry. Current yield from U.S. cotton crops is about twice that of 1950, or
about one and one-third bales per acre (a bale equals about 500 pounds).

While cotton is relatively easy to grow, there can be significant vari-
ability in the quality of cotton, which is a major factor in how cotton is
priced. Cotton is graded by the U.S. Department of Agriculture (USDA), and
each grade expresses cotton's quality with regard to color, brightness, and
amount of foreign matter. Coarse cotton is used for cloth such as denim,
while premium cotton is used to make soft sheets and shirts.

DEMAND

The USDA forecasts record foreign cotton demand in 2005–2006 for the
seventh consecutive year. During this period, the USDA reports that cotton
consumption has risen almost 50 percent—from 74.4 million bales from
1998–1999 to an estimated 110.9 million bales for 2005–2006.

Leading the increase in foreign consumption has been China's mill
usage, which climbed by more than 26 million bales during the past seven
years. The USDA estimated cotton mill use of 45 million bales for China in
2004–2005 and other mill use of 66 million bales (an increase of 10 million
bales over the past seven years). In total, the USDA forecasts China's share
of world consumption will be 41 percent in 2005–2006, compared with a 25
percent share in 1998–1999. The next-largest consumers of cotton production are India, Pakistan, and Turkey, which represent 14 percent, 10 percent, and 6 percent of world consumption, respectively (2003–2004 USDA
estimates).

The USDA projects total U.S. demand for cotton will rise 6 percent year over year to a record 22.3 million bales in 2005–2006. On the other hand, the USDA projects a decline in U.S. cotton mill use—from 6.7 million bales in 2004–2005 to 5.9 million bales in 2005–2006, the lowest level since 1984–1985.

Driving the decline is a lack of growth in the export of cotton products and a simultaneous rise in imports of cotton textiles and apparel. Cotton textile imports rose 11 percent over previous-year levels during the first 11 months of 2005, says the USDA, while shipments of cotton textile products during the same period were only slightly higher than previous-year levels. Over the past decade, production of U.S. cotton cloth has declined by almost half, as more and more production has moved to low-wage foreign countries.

SUPPLY

Worldwide production of cotton in 2005–2006 is expected to decline somewhat from its previous-year record high of 120.4 million bales, double the level produced 25 years ago (USDA). But at almost 114 million bales (USDA), 2005–2006 production levels will still be 24.9 million bales higher than five years earlier.

Together, the world's biggest cotton producers—China, the United States, and India—represent 60 percent of world output, a leadership role they have been expanding. These three also account for 80 percent of the world's increased production over the past five years.

The USDA forecasts that the U.S. cotton supplies will reach 29.3 million bales in 2005–2006, a 9 percent increase over the previous year and the highest supply level since 1965–1966. This supply number takes into account beginning stocks (5.5 million bales), imports (40,000 bales), and a projected U.S. cotton crop of 23.7 bales, a slight increase over the 2004–2005 crop of 23.3 million bales. Combined, the 2004–2005 and 2005–2006 crops are the largest on record for the United States, according to the USDA.

Driving these record production levels have been excellent growing conditions in the U.S. cotton belt. Cotton requires a long growing season with plentiful sun and water, followed by dry weather for harvesting, when cotton bolls are the most vulnerable to damage from wind and rain.

TRADING

Cotton futures trade on the New York Cotton Exchange, which is a division of the New York Board of Trade (NYBOT) and the Bolsa de Mercadorias &

Futures (BM&F) in Rio de Janeiro. Cotton yarn futures trade on the Central Japan Commodity Exchange (CCOM) and the Osaka Mercantile Exchange (OME). All cotton futures contracts, with the exception of India, have been traded in U.S. dollars since the abolition of the gold standard in 1973.

The New York Cotton Exchange's futures contracts call for delivery of 50,000 pounds of net weight (about 100 bales) of No. 2 cotton with a quality rating of Strict Low Middling and a staple length of 12/32 inch. The Cotton No. 2 contract is priced in cents and hundredths of a cent per pound, with each price tick valued at $5.

Contract delivery is accepted in Galveston and Houston, New Orleans, Memphis, and Greenville/Spartanburg (South Carolina); and the five active delivery months are March, May, July, October, and December. The current month plus one or more of the next 23 succeeding months are available for trade (e.g., a March 2006 contract could be traded as early as April 2006).

Cotton-classing components covered by the New York Cotton Exhange's No. 2 cotton futures contracts include color, length, micronaire, and strength. The contract allows delivery of only white grades of good middling to low middling, as well as light spotted grades of good middling to middling. The basic fiber length allowed is 1/32 inch, with a minimum 11/32 inch at commercial discount and a maximum of 13/32 at a premium. Strength is quoted in "Gram per Tex."

The cotton industry uses the No. 2 cotton futures contract as its primary tool to hedge cotton prices in purchases or sales of cotton. Cotton futures and the cash, or spot, market in cotton have a strong relationship and generally move in tandem over time. Moreover, there are generally differences between the cash and futures prices of cotton, differences that may widen or narrow, but which converge as the futures contract reaches maturity. With cotton, understanding the difference between basis and futures prices is especially important due to the many pricing variables that can affect the global marketplace for this commodity. Successful hedges require careful examination of the product trading in the cash market, because basis risk cannot be transferred to the futures market.

Another risk associated with futures trading is currency risk—potential losses due to changes in currency values relative to the U.S. dollar when hedging or speculating in currencies other than the U.S. dollar. Historically, the No. 2 cotton futures contract has tended to show negative correlation to the value of the dollar. As the U.S. dollar has fallen, cotton has often risen in price; and conversely, when the U.S. dollar has risen, cotton has generally fallen in price.

Traders in U.S. cotton must also have an understanding of the impact that government support programs can have on cotton trading. From 1950 to the early 1970s, for example, the trading volume of the New York Commodities Exchange was very low, reflecting the U.S. government's policy of maintaining large cotton stocks through the Commodity Credit Corporation (CCC), which bought and sold most of the U.S. cotton, thereby eliminating a need for cotton merchants to hedge against price changes.

Cotton hedgers can make use of a variety of futures and forward contracts in fulfilling hedging and investment strategies. The New York Board of Trade offers the following examples:

Example 1[*]

Scenario: *In April 2001, a cotton grower has planted his acreage and is considering how to best manage his cotton price risk through harvest. The December Cotton No. 2^{SM} futures contract is trading around 50 cents a pound, but the grower is unwilling to assume that the price will not decline by harvest. The grower has planted 1,600 acres to cotton, with an expected yield of 750 pounds per acre, generating expected production of 2,400 bales (each bale contains 500 pounds of cotton; each futures contract covers approximately 100 bales). The grower looks to hedge half his expected harvest using the December futures contract (December contract best approximates the time of expected cotton harvest).*

Strategy: *To manage this price risk, the grower sells 12 December 2001 contracts (1,200 bales / 100 bales per contract = 12 contracts).*

4/2/01—sell 12 Dec 2001 futures at 49.30 cts./lb. (4930)

Result: *In early November, cotton prices have (as the grower feared) declined, and the grower chooses to sell his cash cotton at a fixed price. Simultaneously, he unwinds his futures hedge by buying the position back from the market:*

11/1/01—buy 12 Dec 2001 futures at 30.03 cts./lb. (3003)

The grower's futures hedge strategy has generated a futures profit of $115,620, calculated as follows:

12 contracts × [(Selling price less purchase price) × $5 (Tick value)]

or

---

[*]Reprinted by permission of the New York Board of Trade® (NYBOT®), New York's original futures exchange and the global marketplace for "soft" commodities.

$$12 \times [(4930 - 3003) \times \$51 = \$115,620$$

The grower's futures hedge has generated a profit of $115,620, and the grower can use this trading profit to offset the lower selling price he obtained by selling his cash cotton in November, since the cash price has declined as the futures price fell. While the movement of the two prices is not likely to have been exactly equal, the hedging profit will offset some or all of the lower cash selling price, thus achieving the grower's goal of managing his price risk on this portion of his cotton production.

Alternate Strategy: *The grower could have managed his price risk by purchasing Cotton Put Options, as follows:*

4/2/01—purchase 12 Dec 2001

48 cent puts at 315 premium, total cost of $18,900

$$(315 \times \$5 \times 12) = \$18,900$$

Alternate Result (price declines): *By expiration in early November, the Dec 2001 futures contract price has fallen to 32.78, and the value of the 48 cent puts has increased. The grower could sell his cash cotton at a fixed price and simultaneously close out his options hedge position as follows:*

11/9/01—sell 12 Dec 2001 48 puts at 1523 premium,
receiving total of $91,380

The grower's option hedge would have returned a profit (before trading costs) of $72,480 (premium received minus premium paid), which would partially offset the lower selling price received for his cotton. Assume that the grower's cash selling price is equal to the futures price; this means his total return for the portion of his crop hedged with options was its cash selling price of $196,680 (1,200 bales, or 600,000 pounds, times 32.78 cents per pound) plus its option hedge profit of $72,480, or $269,160.

Example 2

Scenario: *In early May, an investor has reached the conclusion that cotton prices have bottomed out and are due to increase over the next several months.*

Strategy: *The investor establishes a long position in the December futures contract:*

5/2/02—buy 3 Dec 2002 futures at 38.82 cts./lb. (3882)

Result: *By mid-June, the investor is proven correct as cotton futures prices have increased, and the investor decides to liquidate his (or her) position by selling out the three lots purchased in early May.*

6/17/02—sell 3 Dec 2002 futures at 43.99 cts./lb. (4399)

Since each cotton futures contract represents 50,000 pounds of cotton, and since the future contract price is quoted in terms of U.S. cents per pound, each point has a value of $5.00; the investor's return from this trading strategy is a profit (before trading fees) of $7,755, calculated as follows:

3 contracts × [(Sale price less purchase price) × $5 (Tick value)]

or

$$3 \times (4399 - 3882) \times \$5 = \$7,755.$$

In choosing to take a long market position in the futures contract, the investor accepted an unknown amount of risk from the possibility that the December futures price could decline rather than rise.

Alternate Strategy: *The investor purchases call options instead of futures contracts on the same trading dates as in the futures example.*

5/2/02—buy 3 Dec 2002 40 cent calls at 1.90 premium,
total cost of $2,850 (190 × $5 × 3)

6/17/02—sell 3 Dec 2002 40 cent calls at 562 premium,
receiving $8,430 (562 × $5 × 3)

Alternative Result: *This option strategy would have generated a return (before trading fees) of $5,580, while taking advantage of the fact that the investor's risk was limited to the amount paid to purchase the options, or $2,850.*

CHAPTER 19

Orange Juice

OVERVIEW

Oranges are technically a kind of berry and originated in India, where the orange, called *na rangi*, was bitter. The Indian orange was one of three major varieties of oranges: sweet oranges, sour oranges, and mandarin oranges.

Today, growers produce millions of tons of sweet oranges annually for commercial consumption, including Hamlin, Jaffa, navel, Pineapple, and Valencia oranges. Sour oranges are used for commercial consumption as well, but primarily for marmalade and in liqueurs.

Like cocoa and coffee, orange production has to be planned years in advance. It requires an extended development time and long-term commitments of land and labor. Oranges come from semitropical, nondeciduous trees that take about 3 to 5 years to bear fruit and 15 to 20 years to reach peak production. Groves are productive for 60 to 70 years; but productivity begins to decline after trees reach 30 years of age.

Even after a grove is established, producers remain vulnerable to a variety of potential price shocks. The number of trees bearing fruit, the ages of the trees, the fruit yield per tree, the size of the fruit, fruit droppage, the juice yield per orange, and loss of trees due to weather or disease can all be important factors in determining a grove's yield and the prices that its oranges will command.

Raw oranges mature in Florida over a nine-month period, commencing in September and lasting through May. Early and midseason oranges mature between September and February, while Valencias (late season) are harvested from late February through June. Of the three seasonal varieties of oranges, it is the Valencia that is most significant for concentrate processing. Early and midseason oranges are high in acid content and low in sugar, while the Valencia's proportional content of acid and sugar is the exact opposite. These juices are blended together, under the strict quality standards and supervision of the Florida Citrus Commission, and, after processing, are converted into frozen orange juice concentrate or chilled single-strength orange juice.

It takes two to four medium-sized oranges to produce one cup of juice. But before juice is extracted from an orange, orange oil is recovered from the peel for use in flavors, perfumes, and cleaning agents. As with cotton, no part of an orange is wasted during production. Following juice extraction, which represents about 50 percent of an orange's weight, the remaining peel, pulp, and seeds are dried and made into cattle feed.

Brazil—the world's leading producer of orange juice—is also the biggest exporter of orange juice. Brazil's frozen concentrate orange juice (FCOJ) industry began developing in the 1960s and grew quickly to where FCOJ became the country's third-largest agricultural export after soybeans and coffee.

Most oranges for U.S.–produced FCOJ are grown in Florida. The concentrate is blended from two types of Florida oranges: early and midseason oranges harvested from October through March and later-maturing Valencia oranges that are harvested from April through June. When there is not enough U.S. production to meet domestic demand, imports of FCOJ are needed. Those imports come primarily (but not exclusively) from Brazil. But the quality of the blend is generally unchanged regardless of where the oranges are from.

The U.S. marketing season for FCOJ begins December 1 and continues through November 30, while the Brazilian season extends from June 1 to May 31. The freeze season in Florida runs from December through March, and drought season in Brazil stretches from July to November. As a result of this inverse relationship between the growing seasons for the United States and Brazil, the FCOJ market, which relies heavily on United States and Brazilian production, is a year-round market.

Unlike Brazil and the United States, whose orange crops are grown primarily for processing, other orange-growing countries utilize their crops for the fresh produce market. Juice processing is a residual use of oranges.

DEMAND

The U.S. Department of Agriculture (USDA) forecasts the U.S. consumption of orange juice in the marketing year 2005–2006 at about 962,000 tons, which continues a downward trend. Meanwhile, retail prices for orange juice climbed about 3 percent from the same period a year earlier.

Brazil's orange juice consumption is forecasted at only 21,000 tons for the marketing year 2005–2006, a decline of 2 percent. The USDA reports that Brazilian consumers prefer squeezing their juice from fresh oranges each day, rather than buying orange juice.

The USDA anticipates that demand for orange juice in China during the marketing year 2005–2006 will stagnate due to the rising cost of imported juice. China's main supplier of orange juice is Brazil, where juice prices have soared 50 percent over the previous-year level. This has made it more cost effective for Chinese juicing companies to utilize domestic oranges for juicing. This is not a long-term solution, however, as most oranges produced in China are better suited to fresh consumption than juicing.

SUPPLY

Orange juice supply is especially vulnerable to the vicissitudes of Mother Nature. Freezes and frost periodically afflict the Florida orange market, while Brazilian production can suffer from drought. Freezing can damage or destroy existing fruit and damage flowers, thereby stunting the next season's potential output. Drought can also retard or damage buds, damaging the next season's harvest as well. In addition, Florida's groves are subject to damage from hurricanes, which can destroy production for an entire grove.

Other factors that can impact orange juice supply include processing capacity, disease, and strength of the U.S. dollar. If large quantities of oranges are pushed on to the market by adverse weather, for example, processing capacity may be unable to accommodate the increases. And because FCOJ is priced in U.S. dollars, a spike in the dollar can drive up juice prices in Europe and other markets.

Although other regions of the United States and other Central and South American countries compete in the orange market, Florida and Brazil dominate the market. Together, Brazil and the United States account for about 89 percent of world output for selected major producers for orange juice, according to a recent USDA report. Brazil alone accounts for 39 percent of the world's orange production, followed by the United States, which represents 23 percent of production (*CRB Commodity Yearbook 2003–2004*). Brazil leads the world in orange juice exports (1.4 million tons in 2005–2006/USDA forecast). It provides 30 to 50 percent of the FCOJ consumed in the United States and is also a major source for Canadian and European supplies.

The United States, on the other hand, consumes most of its orange juice production. The largest single export market for U.S. orange juice exports (75,000 tons in 2005–2006/USDA estimate) is Canada (54 percent of export total), followed by the European Union (25 percent).

The biggest producer of oranges in the United States is the state of Florida, whose orange industry has been one of the most rapidly expanding and changing commodity systems in U.S. agribusiness. Florida's production has grown from 10 million boxes in the 1920s to about 158 million boxes in 2005–2006 (USDA). The cultivation of this crop is concentrated in a few major producing counties in Florida, which produce about 75 percent of the total U.S. crop. Normally, 95 percent of Florida's orange crop is processed for orange juice.

Florida's all-orange production in 2005–2006 was forecast to be about 7.1 million tons, a 6 percent increase over the 2004–2005 crop. Prior to Hurricane Wilma, Florida's 2005–2006 orange production had been expected to rise about 27 percent from the previous year.

The development of the Florida processing industry created a need for some type of coordinated production, processing, and marketing operations in order that the consumer could have a consistent quantity and quality of orange concentrate despite extremely volatile fluctuations in production and price. The Florida orange industry is a very tightly knit group, and it is nearly impossible for any individual grower or processor to operate independently of industry policies. Perhaps the most visible evidence of the degree of coordination and integration within the orange industry is the complex network of cooperatives. There are many types of cooperatives, whose members may include growers, processors, private companies, and other co-ops.

Today, cooperative agreements offer orange growers several advantages, including a guaranteed market price for a grower's crop and a guaranteed minimum price equal to the Florida Canners Association average-price-per-pound solid. Most cooperatives work on a "price pool" basis. The cooperative keeps a record of the "solid content" of each grower's deliveries. The cooperative does not price each grower's oranges as they are delivered to the cooperative or processor, but rather pools all the sales over a time period that covers the early varieties for one period and the late varieties for another.

In this way, each member of the cooperative receives the average price of the pool for the pound-solid quantities he or she delivered. It is no longer important to the grower whether or not his or her crop is delivered at a high-priced or low-priced period of the harvest. The pool enables each member to average out the price swings that can take place within a crop year.

The advantages to the processors are guaranteed supply of a certain number of boxes of oranges; pool contracts that keep average procurement costs in line with competitors' procurement costs (since all are related to the Florida Canners Association price); and payment flexibility, in that processors do not have to pay the growers until payment is received for their output.

Processors have devised many arrangements to improve their coordination within the total Florida orange system. In order to improve procurement operations by maintaining a flow of raw material to the plant, some processors have resorted to backward integration in the form of actual grove ownership or leasing of orange groves.

Processors have also attempted to reduce the market uncertainties affecting their output by entering into retail volume contracts, whereby, for example, a processor would "can" its output for a major food retailer under the retailer's product label.

Advantages of the retail volume-shipment contracts to the processors include guarantees of a market for a certain volume of a processor's orange concentrate, receipt of storage payment from the retailer on invoiced merchandise that remains in the processors' warehouses, guarantees of approximately equal monthly shipments of processors' products, and guarantees of prompt payment for invoiced concentrate.

The retailer also benefits from the arrangement in that the retailer gets guaranteed delivery of specified quantities of frozen orange concentrate and free storage on all concentrate invoiced until January 15 of the season. Moreover, the retailer is guaranteed a quality USDA-inspected product, and the retailer's cost is guaranteed to be no more than that of any other retailer on the date of invoicing or shipment.

TRADING

Futures for frozen concentrated orange juice trade on the New York Commodities Exchange division of the New York Board of Trade (NYBOT). The contract, which has been the primary hedging vehicle for the citrus industry since 1966, calls for delivery of 15,000 pounds of orange solids (3 percent more or less) from Florida and/or Brazil only. The new FCOJ-A contract, which began trading May 1995, replaces the previous FCOJ-1 futures contract and allows hedgers to buy or sell a contract to make delivery through exchange-licensed warehouses in Florida, New Jersey, Delaware, and California. It is priced in terms of cents per pound.

A second contract on the NYBOT—the FCOJ-B contract—has no specified country of origin. For most of its life, however (all but a day and a half), this contract trades as a Differential contract (FCOJ-Diff).

The only variables between FCOJ-A and FCOJ-B contracts are price and contract month (date, size, and standards are identical). Buyers and sellers in the exchange's open outcry auction determine the contract's price minute-to-minute, and the resulting price fluctuations are instantly disseminated throughout the world. These changing prices become the most reliable benchmark for the global cash market in orange juice.

PART SIX

Speculating in Agricultural Commodities and Meats

CHAPTER 20

Grain

OVERVIEW

The production, distribution, and processing of grain and oilseeds by U.S. firms represent a multi-billion-dollar industry. This chapter focuses on the most important of these crops: wheat, corn, and soybeans. We will also touch on lesser crops, such as barley, sorghum grain, oats, flaxseed, rye—but only briefly. It should be noted, however, that many of the major grain companies also trade in these lesser crops.

WHEAT

Wheat is divided into five classes: hard winter wheat, soft red winter wheat, hard spring wheat, durum, and white wheat.

1. *Hard winter wheat.* Represents the largest wheat class and is grown in the Plains states: Colorado, Kansas, Nebraska, Oklahoma, Texas. Kansas is by far the largest grower. This class of wheat has high protein content and is primarily used for bread and quality baking flour. It is deliverable on the Kansas City Board of Trade.

2. *Soft red winter wheat.* A lower protein wheat, which is grown in the central and southern states. It is the second-largest wheat class in terms of production. It is primarily used in cookie and cake manufacturing. This class of wheat is deliverable on the Chicago Board of Trade.

3. *White wheat.* Similar to soft red winter wheat in protein and usage. Grown in the Northwest and exported primarily out of the Pacific Coast.

4. *Hard spring wheat.* The highest protein wheat produced. Used in quality breads. Produced in the north central states: Minnesota, North Dakota, South Dakota. This grade is deliverable on the Minneapolis Grain Exchange.

5. *Durum.* Used in producing semolina, which is used in the production of macaroni (pasta) products. Grown in the same area as the hard spring wheat.

The winter wheats are planted in the fall and harvested in the summer, while the spring wheats are planted in the spring and harvested in late summer. The majority of domestic grain is either exported or milled into flour. The remainder of the usage is divided between feed and seed. The major exporters are the Russian Federation (and other countries of the former Soviet Union, such as Ukraine), China, Japan, Eastern Europe, Brazil, Egypt, Iran, and South Korea. Other major exporting countries are Argentina, Canada, Australia, and the members of the European Union.

CORN

The two major classes of corn are yellow corn and white corn, with yellow being by far the predominant class. The major growing areas are the central states, that is, Iowa, Illinois, Minnesota, and Nebraska. Corn is planted in the spring and is harvested in the fall. Domestically, the primary use of corn is for feed, either directly to livestock or following a milling process. Processed corn is also used for human consumption and for the production of high-fructose corn syrup. Another potential market for corn is in the production of ethanol for gasohol. The major export markets for corn are Japan, Russia, Spain, West Germany, Italy, Poland, Taiwan, and Korea.

SOYBEANS

The classes of soybeans are yellow, green, brown, and black, with the predominant class being yellow. The major growing areas for soybeans are the midwestern and south central states, and the leading producers are Illinois and Iowa. Soybeans are planted in the late spring and harvested in late fall.

The soybean has little commercial use in itself; however, processing yields soybean meal and oil. Soybean meal is a high-protein livestock feed that is also being used increasingly as a protein and mineral fortifier in baking goods and sausage meats.

Soybean oil, after being refined, is added to vegetable shortenings, margarines, and salad oils. It also is used in oil paints and varnishes.

The major export markets for soybeans are Japan, the Netherlands, West Germany, and Spain. Brazil and Argentina are also major soybean producers.

STORAGE, MERCHANDISING, AND EXPORT

The following represents an overview of the services provided by the elevator, merchandiser, and exporter and identifies certain common industry practices and risks. It must be pointed out that the industry is extremely complex and that the following represents a very general broad-brush approach.

Elevators

Country Elevators.   Grain that moves into merchandising channels is normally first purchased from the producer or stored for the producer by a country elevator. The grain is usually brought to the elevator by truck. A sample is weighed and graded, and the grain is either purchased or stored by the elevator. If stored for the producer, the elevator issues a warehouse receipt. Normally, the weighing, sampling, and inspection at country elevators is not done by individuals employed by official agencies. The grading of the grain is critical, as prices are based on the grade. Such things as test weight per bushel, damaged kernels, foreign material, moisture content, and so on, are considered when determining the appropriate grade.

In addition to grade, wheat is also classified by protein level, with the higher proteins usually being traded at premiums. Wheat and corn are graded from number 1 to number 5 plus a United States sample grade that does not meet the grades 1 through 5 requirements. Grade number 1 is the most favorable. Soybeans are classified by grades 1 through 4, with a United States sample grade for those that do not meet the grades 1 through 4 requirements. During the period of time that the grain is stored, it is important for the elevator to maintain the quality of the grain, as it is responsible for delivering to the receipt holder a specific amount and quality of grain. In addition to grain storage, the country elevator provides drying, cleaning, scalping, and automatic sampling, for which fees are normally charged. The elevator also uses its drying and cleaning equipment to improve the grade of grain it purchases for its own account, which enables it to receive a better price on resale.

Two major risks that are associated with the storage of grain are quality deterioration and the possibility of the grain being destroyed, that is, through fire and elevator explosion. The maintenance of grain quality and condition is a function of warehouse management and proper equipment and is probably best evaluated by observing the experience of the warehouse and through checking with other firms in the industry. According to our industry sources, deterioration of the grain through explosion, fire, and so on, can be covered by insurance and can also be reduced by proper operating procedures. Research is actively being done on the causes of grain explosions; and equipment is being designed to reduce the levels of grain dust, to better ventilate elevators, and to better measure concentration of gases and vapors. The insurance that is maintained should cover the value of both the real estate and grain, as well as the business interruption.

Terminal, Subterminal, and River Elevators.   The next step in the merchandising chain usually involves the grain moving directly into the processing industries; or being sold as feed; or being sold to terminal, subterminal, or river elevators. These elevators usually have a larger storage capacity and more efficient grain handling equipment than the country elevators and are situated on major transportation lines. These elevators serve the purpose of aggregating grain in convenient locations for bulk movement into export channels or domestic processing. Purchases are usually made from country elevators or merchandisers, and grain is stored for merchandisers and processors.

When the grain leaves the country elevator, it is weighed and graded before a bill of lading is issued by the carrier. If the elevator is not an official station, the grain is again weighed and graded en route at an official station. The official weight and grade are then sent along with a draft to the terminal elevators. The drafts are pro forma, calling for a 90 percent payment of the contract price. When the grain is received at the terminal elevator, it is again weighed and graded, and the remainder of the draft is paid. The drafts are normally documentary sight drafts and are collected through banking channels. The use of a negotiable bill of lading allows the grain to be traded frequently while en route.

The terminal elevators represent the major inland storage facilities, and certain elevators are designated as good for delivery on the grain exchanges. Grain can be received at these elevators by truck, rail, or barge; and one important factor in their success is the equipment and capacity they have to receive and load-out grain. Normally at these elevators, grain is sampled, weighed, and graded by either employees of official agencies or by employees licensed under the United States Grain Standards Act. When these as well as other requirements are met, the weights and grades are considered official and are used in conducting trade. The terminal elevators provide the same services as country elevators, and the major risks associated with storage are the same.

Exchange Elevators. Each one of the three-grain exchanges has designated elevators that are acceptable for delivery of the particular grain being traded. Before an elevator is declared "regular" for delivery on the Chicago Board of Trade (CBOT), it must be inspected by the CBOT. The exchange may require that all grain in the elevator be removed and inspected and graded and that new receipts be issued. The elevator must also have appropriate rail facilities and must have adequate equipment for the receiving, handling, and shipping of grain in bulk. Appropriate bonds and insurance must be in place, and the warehouse must be in good financial standing. Records must be maintained of all grain received and delivered daily by grade and of grain remaining in store at the end of the week.

The warehouses are inspected at least twice a year by the exchange. The warehouses that are designated as "regular" for delivery of corn, wheat, and soybeans are located in switching districts in Chicago (47.3 million bushels), Toledo (45.4 million bushels), and St. Louis (16.9 million bushels) and are elevators of the major grain merchandisers and cooperatives. All warehouse receipts that are eligible for delivery on the CBOT must be registered with the exchange, and the exchange verifies signatures.

In order for a warehouse to be "regular" for delivery on the Kansas City Exchange, it must be licensed as a public warehouse by the federal government, or Kansas, or Missouri; and its capacity must be at least 100 bushels. The elevator must have appropriate facilities and rail connections and be of unquestioned financial standing. At a minimum, its net worth should be 15 cents per bushel, based on aggregate capacity. The elevator must be appropriately bonded and insured. The elevator's status as "regular" for delivery must be renewed annually. Total capacity for deliverable grain is 84.2 million bushels.

Export Elevators. The main function of the export elevator is to move the grain from the inland transportation, that is, rail, barge, or truck, and place it on ships. A fee is charged for this service, which is known in the industry as "fobbing." The fee is a per bushel charge; and, therefore, the elevator's capacity to unload and load the grain is crucial. To increase utilization, elevators will enter into throughput agreements with shippers, in which the shipper agrees to process a certain amount of grain through the elevator. Storage represents a minor portion of the operations of the export elevator as income to the export vessel. As the grain leaves the elevator and falls into the vessel, it is weighed and graded, based on a sample; and a mates receipt is issued. The mates receipt is the title document. The mates receipt is then exchanged for a bill of lading. Export elevators provide the same services as the terminal and country elevators.

Merchandising

An integral part of elevator operations is the merchandising of grain. The aim of the elevator is to use its capacity to the fullest extent. This is done by turning over the grain as quickly as possible and only storing grain when it is necessary from a marketing viewpoint or in order to use existing capacity. Ideally, the elevator, when purchasing grain, would like to immediately be able to sell the grain at a price that would cover its handling charges and provide a profit. This is not always possible, however, as the elevator must be able to service its customers and is, therefore, forced to buy when they are ready to sell. In this event, the elevator has the ability to hedge its purchase on one of the grain exchanges. Normally, elevators will be constantly in touch with other elevators and merchandisers, receiving bids for grain to be delivered at specific locations at specific times. The elevator can then discount transportation and interest charges and know what to bid for grain. If there are no active buyers, the elevator can use the prices quoted on the grain exchanges as the base from which to discount transportation and interest costs. As the price of grain can be extremely volatile and as the elevators and merchandisers trade large amounts of grains in relation to their capital, their merchandising and hedging policies are of critical importance.

Merchandising Risk

There appear to be three aspects to the merchandising risk: credit, contract cancellations, and transportation risks.

1. *Credit.* Generally speaking, supplier credit is not extended in the industry. Domestic sales are normally on sight draft against documents. The drafts are drawn for 90 percent of the contract value and are accompanied by bills of lading, weight certificate, certificate of grade, and other necessary shipping documents. These drafts are normally collected through bank channels; thus the seller does not release the title document (bill of lading) until the draft has been paid.

   This drafting procedure reduces the credit risk associated with domestic transactions. The credit exposure taken by the seller is reduced to the 10 percent of the invoice price not covered by the draft. This 10 percent is paid by the buyer after weighing and sampling the grain.

While in theory this 10 percent should be outstanding for a short period of time, transportation and paperwork delays may, according to industry sources, cause this payment to be deferred for a number of months.

Bulk shipments are normally made by rail or barge. A normal hopper carries 3,500 bushels, while a barge will carry 43,000 bushels. Rail shipments of 75 cars are now being made, due to transportation discounts; and multibarge shipments may be sold to substantial customers. The significance of this 10 percent exposure is obviously dependent upon the capital of the selling firm and the size of the transaction.

International transactions are normally shipped on confirmed or advised letters of credit (sight or time) or cash against documents. If time drafts under letters of credit are used, the drafts are normally discounted without recourse by a bank. Credit exposure is therefore limited to the instance in which the advising bank refuses to negotiate drafts although properly presented under a letter of credit. This exposure represents a sovereign and foreign bank risk that is similar to the risk when shipping CAD (cash against documents).

2. *Contract cancellations.* Grain companies commit themselves far in advance of shipment dates to purchase and sell grain. These commitments are normally either hedged or done on a back-to-back basis. Elevators may contract to purchase grain from producers in advance of the harvest or contract to purchase grain from the other elevators or merchandisers for deferred delivery.

   In the event that the supplier of the grain defaults, the firm will have to either buy back its hedge or go into the open market and buy the grain. In a rising market, generally speaking, a loss will be sustained equal to the difference between the price at which the buyer contracted to purchase the grain and the open market price. In the event of a buyer's default, the firm could suffer a loss in a declining market.

3. *Transportation.* The ability to transport grain by the cheapest and most efficient manner is critical to a firm's profitability. The responsibility for providing transportation is dependent upon the terms of sales. The predominant modes of domestic transportation are barge and rail. Hopper cars are the most frequently used to obtain transportation when needed. If the terms of sale require that the grain be in a railcar at a Gulf of Mexico port at a specific time, and due to a car shortage a timely delivery is not made, a default may exist. In order to reduce the risk of car shortages and also reduce rail charges, the large firms will lease or buy hopper cars.

   The same situation exists with barge transportation, and the larger firms also maintain a fleet of barges. In addition to shortages of transportation, a risk that may be lessened by controlling railcars and barges, delays in the transportation system represent a separate risk. Barge transportation may be delayed due to low water levels or congestion on the rivers. Rail delays occur primarily when export elevators are unable to process the railcars quickly enough. The cars get backed up, and a rail embargo may be declared.

The inland transportation must also be coordinated with the arrival of the export vessel, as demurrage will be incurred if the grain is not in place when the vessel is in port and will also be incurred if the grain arrives early and the railcars or barge cannot be unloaded. Demurrage charges on large shipments can run up to $8 million to $10 million per day. In addition, the firm's capacity to load large quantities of grain at a given time will improve margins, as freight rates will be reduced.

As an example, railroads have recently introduced discounted rates for movement of grain in units of 75 cars. A firm that is able to take advantage of this discount can be more competitive than a smaller firm. The major grain firms have departments whose sole responsibility is coordinating transportation.

In summary, it appears that the major risks associated with elevator and merchandising operations are elevator explosion and fires, which are reduced by proper insurance coverage; grain deterioration, which can be controlled by adequate operating procedures; and inventory losses due to price fluctuations, which can be mitigated by a well-conceived hedging program. Contract defaults also represent a potential risk to a firm; however, defaults are reportedly rare in the industry.

The risk associated with receivables, which is common in any industry, is generally reduced to 10 percent of the invoice volume for domestic sales, due to their drafting procedure, and normally consists of a country and foreign bank exposure on foreign sales when unconfirmed letters of credit and CAD terms are used.

While the industry has developed methods of controlling their exposure to inventory price fluctuations and credit risks associated with their sales, such external factors as weather and transportation are out of its control. Firms within the industry are therefore subject to reduced volume and lower margins due to a poor harvest or transportation delays. As the industry is very competitive, it is important that the grain delivery system be run in an efficient manner; or a firm may have the normally thin margins eliminated through excessive demurrage charges, grain deterioration during transportation, and so on.

As with any industry, the risk involved in this industry must be applied to individual firms; thus contract defaults or even the 10 percent credit exposure on receivables may be significant, depending on the size of the firm in relation to the contracts in which it deals.

PROCESSORS

The processing of grain is becoming concentrated to a greater degree with the large agribusiness firms. Discussions with firms in the industry indicate that the future of the industry lies with the larger firms and that the single processing firm is a dying breed.

Flour Milling

The majority of wheat is milled for flour. Mills are normally established to process particular classes of wheat, which flour is used for different purposes. Hard winter and hard spring wheat produce a flour suitable for quality breads, due to its high protein content. Soft winter wheat is used to produce flour for baking and cookie and cracker manufacturers, while durum wheat produces semolina, which is used in the manufacture of pasta products. The extraction rate from the wheat is approximately 72 percent, with the remaining 28 percent classified as "millfeed," which is used in animal feed. The millers will purchase grain directly from farmers, elevators, or merchandisers and normally have elevator capacity at the mill to store the grain prior to processing. The grain is normally purchased on sight draft terms from the elevators and merchandisers. The flour is then sold to bakers or jobbers on draft or open-account terms of up to 60 days or, for the larger firms, retailed under their own name.

Milling firms used to book business out to 120 days, which did not include carrying charges to the buyer. In the recent environment of high interest rates, the free carrying charge period has been reduced to 60 days. The wheat futures markets are actively used by the firms to hedge inventory and purchase and sales commitments. While there is not a futures market for flour, there is an active physical market with prices quoted for the various types of flour. The price of flour is affected by the price of wheat as well as by the price of millfeed, which is also traded in physical markets. If the millfeed market is particularly strong, the miller may be able to reduce the price of flour in relation to the income being earned by millfeed sales. One other major factor in a mill's operation is transportation costs. The mill is affected by the cost of transporting grain to its facilities and also the cost of shipping the flour and millfeeds to its buyers. If the firm is able to take advantage of freight discounts through bulk loading, it will better be able to maintain its margin.

Corn Milling

Two processing methods are used for corn: dry milling and wet milling. The dry milling process produces grits, cereal products, feed, meal, oil, and industrial products. The wet milling process produces, in addition to the products just mentioned, high-fructose corn syrup, which is used as a substitute for sugar. Corn will normally produce about 66 percent starch, which is used in making the syrup, 30 percent feed materials, and 3 percent oils. The feed products and high-fructose corn syrup, while not traded on a futures exchange, are traded actively in physical markets.

Soybean Processing

The processing of soybeans results in soybean meal and soybean oil, both of which are traded on the Chicago Board of Trade. Trade standards are maintained for soybean meal according to the trading rules of the National Soybeans Processors Association (NSPA). The meal is used primarily as a livestock and poultry feed and is both consumed domestically and exported. The soybean oil that is initially extracted from the soybean must be degummed and refined before it is used for edible or industrial purposes. Grade and quality standards are established by the NSPA for crude soybean oil and crude degummed soybean oil. The refined oil is primarily used in food processing, although there are industrial uses in the production of soap, varnish, paint, and so on.

It is estimated that out of a 60-pound bushel of soybeans, the processor gets between 10 and 11 pounds of oil and between 47 and 48 pounds of meal. The basic profitability of a soybean processing operation is reflected in the price relationship between the bean and the meal and oil. This relationship is known as the "crushing margin." A wide crushing margin will result in a high utilization of crushing capacity, while a small margin will cause cutbacks in production. World markets determine the prices of the bean, oil, and meal; and it is therefore difficult for a company to control its margins. Due to the potential for sharp price swings in the bean, oil, and meal markets, firms normally hedge on the Chicago Board of Trade.

Risks

Some of the risks associated with the processors are similar to those identified with elevator operators. As both the price of the raw material (corn, wheat, and soybeans) and the end product can fluctuate widely, open positions represent a risk. It is therefore useful to understand the company's hedging policy with regard to its inventory and forward commitments. Loss through fire and explosion and deterioration of the grain or end product are risks that can be reduced by proper operating procedures and insurance coverage. Selling terms extended by the processor are generally more liberal than those extended by the grain merchandiser, as open account terms of up to 60 days may be granted to the baker, feed manufacturer, and so on, while the processor will purchase on sight draft terms. Transportation costs are also important; and normally, the greater its control over its transportation, the better the firm is able to maintain its margins.

DEMAND

The U.S. Department of Agriculture (USDA) projects that world wheat consumption will rise 2 percent in 2005–2006—from an estimated 609.25 metric million tons (2004–2005) to a record 623.81 million metric tons. Consumption in key countries, such as India and Nigeria, is fueling the new high, as are record consumption levels in the countries of the former Soviet Union and in Europe.

U.S. wheat production, domestic use, and ending stocks will remain largely unchanged in 2005–2006. The USDA forecasts U.S. wheat consumption will rise 1 percent to 32.33 million metric tons from an estimated 31.91 million metric tons in 2004–2005.

World corn consumption is expected to climb to 687.034 million metric tons in 2005–2006 (USDA Feb. 2006) from 680.635 million metric tons estimated for 2004–2005 (USDA Feb. 2006). The United States is the leading user of corn worldwide (228.23 million metric tons/2005–2006 USDA projection), followed by China (134.0 million metric tons/USDA) and the European Union-25 (50.6 million metric tons/USDA).

World soybean use climbed from 189.96 million metric tons in 2003–2004 to an estimated 205.65 metric tons in 2004–2005 (USDA). The USDA projects that demand will increase yet again in 2005–2006, climbing 4 percent to 213.73 metric tons.

South American exporters are expected to capture the biggest share of expanding global trade for soybeans and soybean products, much of which will be directed toward meeting China's skyrocketing demand. Led by Brazil, exports from South America have set record highs every year for nearly a decade, surpassing U.S. foreign trade for the first time in the marketing year 2002–2003 (USDA).

U.S. consumption of soybeans is on the rise as well. The USDA estimates that United States use of soybeans totaled 51.25 million metric tons in 2004–2005, compared with 44.6 million metric tons in 2003–2004. The

USDA forecasts U.S. domestic use of soybeans will rise 25 to 35 million bushels per year, based on steady increases in domestic soybean meal and soybean oil consumption over the next decade.

Even modest increases in domestic use will squeeze supplies available for export, however, with the result that larger price differences between the United States and foreign competitors could develop, driving down soybean exports to 1,040 million bushels by 2013–2014, compared with 1,060 million bushels in 2004–2005. And a strong expansion in foreign exports within the next 10 years could reduce the U.S. global soybean market share to 29 percent, compared with 45 percent in 2002–2003, according to the USDA Economic Research Service.

SUPPLY

The USDA anticipates world wheat production will decline 2 percent in 2005–2006 to 616 million metric tons from an estimated 627 million metric tons in 2004–2005. Even so, projected global wheat production in 2005–2006 is still the second highest in history.

The European Union-25 leads wheat production worldwide with a projected production of 122.94 million metric tons in 2005–2006, followed by China (97 million metric tons), India (72 million metric tons), and the United States (57.28 million metric tons/USDA). Top exporters are the United States (27.22 metric million tons), Australia (16.5 metric million tons), and Canada (16.5 metric million tons).

In 2005–2006, the United States produced 57.3 million metric tons of wheat, compared with 58.7 million metric tons in 2004–2005, a decline of 2 percent (USDA). Exports were also lower due to smaller sales to China.

The USDA anticipates that hard wheat supplies should continue to tighten, with hard red winter (HRW) and hard red spring (HRS) wheat falling to 9- and 10-year winter lows, respectively. The tight supplies of HRW are the result of strong foreign demand, primarily in Nigeria and Iraq; and HRS tightening is due to lower production as well as to strong foreign demand. Soft winter wheat (SRW) exports could improve, on the other hand, due to higher SRW acreage and less competition in soft wheat.

Global corn production is estimated to total 708.38 metric million tons in 2004–2005 versus 623.04 metric million tons in 2003–2004 (USDA). And in 2005–2006, the USDA projects worldwide production of 683.76 metric million tons of corn. Indications are that China's 2005–2006 exports may be larger than anticipated, justifying only a small (3 million tons) increase in U.S. exports (USDA). The United States, which dominates the global corn market, is projected to export a total of 46.99 million metric tons in

2005–2006 (USDA). The second-largest exporter, Argentina, is projected to export 10 million metric tons in 2005–2006 (USDA).

Worldwide soybean production has been on a steady climb, from 186.75 metric tons in 2003–2004 to an estimated 215.3 million metric tons in 2004–2005. And the USDA projects global production of 222.76 million metric tons in 2005–2006. U.S. soybean production, on the other hand, is expected to decline slightly in 2005–2006, from an estimated 85.1 million metric tons in 2004–2005 to a projected 84 million metric tons (USDA). U.S. soybean exports are also expected to decline in 2005–2006—from an estimated 30 million metric tons in 2004–2005 to a projected 24.8 million metric tons in 2005–2006. Record Brazilian production and large new-crop supplies in the rest of South America are helping to pressure U.S. exports (USDA).

TRADING

Whenever grain is purchased or sold, the firm is exposed to a price risk until the transaction is offset by either a physical purchase or a sale or is hedged on one of the futures exchanges. In assessing the risk associated in financing elevators or merchandisers, it is important to understand their hedging policy. Some aspects of a policy that should be addressed are the size of the net position that the firm is willing to maintain, the timing between taking a position and offsetting it with a physical or futures transaction, whether weekend positions are maintained, and the way physical trading is conducted after the exchanges close. While hedging reduces the price risk associated with carrying inventory, it does not eliminate it.

Once a transaction is hedged, the risk exists that the spread between the futures price and the price of the physical grain will move against the firm. This risk can be highlighted by an example:

Example:

April 2
Firm purchases 5,000 bushels of wheat at $4.25/bushel
Firm sells 1 Futures Contract on the CBOT for May delivery for $4.35

April 10

Firm sells 5,000 bushels of wheat at $4.35/bushel	$0.10 profit
Firm buys back May Future at $4.46	– 0.11 loss
Net	$0.01 loss

If the pricing of the physical grain had increased more than the price of the May future, a profit would have been made on the hedge. The potential for disparity between price movements of the physical grain and the futures price is especially evident in the case of wheat, which has the three different classes traded primarily on three different exchanges. While soft winter wheat is primarily traded in Chicago, hard winter wheat in Kansas City, and hard spring wheat in Minneapolis, large transactions in all three classes are hedged in Chicago due to that exchange's larger volume. The prices of the three classes at times move independently, which increases the risk of hedging the hard wheats on CBOT. Prices demonstrate variation in the price movement. In connection with a firm's hedging philosophy, its policy toward hedges that are moving against it should also be discussed.

One other area that should be mentioned in conjunction with a position risk is basis pricing. Grain firms often enter into contracts to buy or sell at a specific spread over a specific contract month on one of the exchanges; for example, purchase of 40 cents over the May Chicago wheat, soft red wheat at the Gulf. Either buying or selling the May Chicago Wheat contract places the hedge. In the preceding examples, a hedge would be placed by selling the May contract. The firm would, therefore, be protected against price movements in the volatile futures market between the time the purchase commitment was made and the physical grain was sold. The price risk is reduced to a basis risk, which is less volatile. Thus, if at the time the grain was sold the basis dropped to 38 cents over the May future, a 2-cent loss would be incurred.

This example requires a thorough understanding of basis—the difference between the local cash price of a commodity and the price of a specific futures contract of the same commodity at any given point in time. In other words, local cash price – futures price = basis.

Local cash price	$2.00
December futures price	–2.20
Basis	–$0.20 December

In this example, the cash price is 20 cents lower than the December futures price. In market "lingo," you'd say the basis is "20 under December." On the other hand, if the cash price were 20 cents higher than the December futures price, you'd say the basis is "20 over December."

Local cash price	$2.20
December futures price	–2.00
Basis	+$0.20 December

Basis, in a sense, is "localizing" a futures price, which represents the world price for grain, and is used as a benchmark in determining the value of grain at the local level. The fact that basis reflects local market conditions means it is influenced by a number of factors, including transportation costs, local supply and demand conditions, interest/storage costs, and handling costs and profit margins.

Paying attention to basis can help futures traders make informed decisions about whether to accept or reject a given price or a particular buyer or seller. Basis can also help clarify when to purchase, sell, or store a crop, depending on whether the current price is stronger or weaker than the average basis. And if basis improves or equals your estimated basis level, it could be a sign to close a hedge by purchasing or selling a commodity. Finally, a quoted basis from a deferred futures month that is more attractive than the nearby futures month could help determine whether, when, and in what delivery month to hedge.

The Chicago Board of Trade offers five characteristics of basis that futures traders need to keep in mind when timing purchases and sales:

1. Basis tends to have a consistent historical pattern.
2. Basis gives a good frame of reference for evaluating current prices.
3. Basis usually weakens around harvest.
4. Basis tends to strengthen after harvest.
5. Basis tends to be consistent even as prices fluctuate.

The CBOT offers the following examples[*] of how to use basis to your advantage.

Example 1: Short Hedger

Because there is a certain amount of "predictability" with basis, it is continually used by the grain industry to make buying and selling decisions. Let's say you have three years of basis history and know the local elevator's basis in early November averages 30 under ($–0.30) the December futures contract. In the spring, you call your elevator and find out he's bidding $1.95 a bushel for corn through a cash forward contract. Delivery is required by November 15. At the time, December corn futures are trading at $2.35. You calculate the basis for early November delivery at 40 under December:

---

[*]Data provided by the Chicago Board of Trade.

Forward cash price Nov. 15 delivery	$1.95
December futures price	− 2.35
Basis	− $0.40 December

Would you take the forward bid? Because the basis is historically weak (−0.40 compared to −0.30) and there is potential for the basis to strengthen, you might consider passing on this bid. However, if you like the current futures price level, you could hedge your price risk using futures. Should the basis strengthen, you would unwind (offset) your futures hedge and sell corn through a forward contract or a spot cash sale.

If you hedge, the expected selling price is:

December futures price	$2.35
Expected basis early November delivery	+(− 0.30)
Expected sale price	$2.05

The only factor that will affect the final sale price will be a change in basis from what is expected. If the basis is stronger than expected, you will receive more than $2.05 for your corn. If the basis is weaker than expected, you will receive less than $2.05.

What if the cash forward bid was $2.15? With December futures at $2.35, this equates to a basis of −0.20.

Forward cash price November 15 delivery	$2.15
December futures price	−2.35
Basis	−$0.20 December

A basis of 20 under is significantly stronger than the historical average of 30 under, so you decide to sell a portion of your anticipated corn crop and take the cash forward bid of $2.15.

Example 2: Long Hedger

Current cash offer for January delivery	$0.28
January futures contract	− 0.25
Current basis	+$0.03

From your years of basis history, you determine that by January the basis is typically about 1/2 cent per pound, or 2½ cents weaker than the present basis. Given current fundamentals, you believe the basis will move toward the historical average. At this point, you can protect your buying price by hedging in the futures market—purchasing futures and later offsetting the futures position—or by entering a forward contract purchasing soybean oil for 28 cents per pound. If you establish a long hedge to protect your buying price level, the expected buying price can be calculated as follows:

Futures price + Expected basis = Expected buying price

Using this formula, you calculate your expected buying price:

$$\$0.25/\text{lb} + (+\$0.005) = \$0.255/\text{lb}$$

This is lower than the cash forward offer of 28 cents per pound. Since the expected buying price with futures is below the cash offer, due to an expected lower basis, you decide to initiate the long hedge and buy January soybean oil futures.

Assume in late December that the futures price has increased to 27 cents. Also, assume that the basis weakens from 3 cents to 1/2 cent. You purchase your January cash soybean oil requirements for 27 cents [($0.27 futures + (+$0.005 basis) = $0.275/lb)] from your supplier. At the same time, you unwind the hedge, or offset the futures position, by selling January futures for 27 cents. The results are shown in Table 20.1.

TABLE 20.1   Long Hedge

Local Cash Price	Futures Market Price	Basis
September		
Cash forward offer @ $0.280/lb	Buys CBOT Jan futures contracts @ $0.250/lb	+$0.030/lb
December		
Buys cash soybean oil @ $0.275/lb	Sells CBOT Jan futures contracts @ $0.270/lb	+$0.005/lb
	$0.020/lb gain	$0.025/lb gain
Net Result		
Cash soybean oil	$0.275/lb	
Futures gain (sells $0.27 – buys $0.25)	0.020/lb	
Net purchase price	$0.255/lb	

Data provided by the Chicago Board of Trade.

CHAPTER 21

Cattle

OVERVIEW

The cycle for cattle production begins with the birth of calves on a cow-producing ranch or farm. Producers breed their herds naturally or, to a lesser extent, through artificial insemination. Naturally bred herds consist on average of one mature bull per 23 cows. While natural breeding still dominates the cattle industry, artificial insemination has increased in recent years. Insemination allows a cattle producer to introduce additional genetic strains into a herd without having to bring in new bulls—strains that can improve the commercial value of the herd.

A cow's gestation period is nine months, and breeding generally takes place in the fall. This eliminates the risk of exposing the calves to cold winter weather and ensures an abundance of green pasture during the calves' first months. Most cows give birth to just one calf, but twins sometimes occur. Cows that do not become pregnant are generally culled from the herd and replaced by new female calves. Each year, 16 percent to 18 percent of cows are culled from a herd on average. Other reasons for elimination include bad teeth, advanced age, drought, or high production costs.

Calves remain with their parent herd for the first six months of their lives. Their sole source of nutrition at birth is milk, a diet that is gradually supplemented with grass and grain. Calves are generally weaned from their mothers when they reach six to eight weeks of age.

A cattle-producing operation requires a certain amount of pasture acreage per cow-calf unit. This acreage, known as stocking, can vary widely, depending on levels of rainfall and on climate. In the Midwest and the East, for example, stockage is typically as low five acres per cow-calf unit, whereas in the West and Southwest, it can be 30 times higher.

Once a calf is weaned, it requires an increasing amount of stockage. A cattle producer may pay a stocker operator to provide calves with access to summer grass, winter wheat, or some type of harvest roughage. Or the producer may simply sell the calves outright to the stocker operator. Calves generally remain with a stocker until they achieve a weight of 600 to 800 pounds, at which point they move on to a feedlot,

Like stocker operations, the services of a feedlot can be purchased, or the feedlot can buy the calves outright. Many feedlots, called *farmer feedlots*, are extensions of a family (or neighborhood) cattle-producing operation and do not feed cattle from outside the local operation. These small feedlots represent the vast majority of feedlots in the United States, but they account for a relatively small portion of total cattle fed at U.S. feedlots.

Large commercial feedlots are defined as having the capacity to serve 1,000 or more head of cattle at one time. These lots are owned by large commercial enterprises for whom feedlot care is the sole focus. These operations commonly have nutritionists and specialized equipment to closely monitor and prescribe feed regimens to meet a cow's dietary needs. This type of expertise allows these operations to customize and streamline the feedlot process, resulting in higher daily weight gains and lower feed conversions.

The menu at feedlots generally consists of grain (corn or wheat), protein supplements (soybeans, cottonseed, or linseed meal), and roughage (alfalfa, silage, or prairie hay). The feedlot phase of the cattle-production process continues until calves reach an optimum balance of weight, muscling, and fat, at which point the animal is considered ready for slaughter. According to the U.S. Department of Agriculture (USDA), the average live slaughter weight in the year 2000 was about 1,222 pounds, and the average carcass weight was 745 pounds.

Cattle producers sell market-ready cows at auction or directly to a packing operation. Packers slaughter the cattle, utilizing every portion of the animal in the fabrication process. Slaughtered cattle provide packers with two primary sources of revenue: the sale of meat and the sale of the remaining carcass parts (fat, bones, blood, glands, and hide).

The slaughtered cow is split down the center and then cut in half or quartered. The hindquarters of the carcass represent 48 percent of the cow's meat, including rump, round, loin, and flank cuts. The front quarters represent the remaining 52 percent of the cow's meat, consisting of rib, chuck, plate, brisket, and foreshank cuts. The majority of the meat is cut into steaks, and the remainder is used for ground beef and stew.

Packers generally sell cow meat in packaged form. The major cuts are vacuum packed and shipped to retailers in boxes, who finish fabricating them. Increasingly, however, the trend is for the packer to finish all the fabricating and to send meat-case-ready cuts to the retailer.

Packers utilize four different pricing methods in negotiating cattle purchases from feedlots. The first, called *formula pricing*, entails a mathematical formula using some other price as a reference, such as the average price of cattle purchased by the plant in the week preceding slaughter.

A second method, *forward contracting*, uses either a basis forward contract or a flat forward contract. In the case of a basis forward contract, a packer offers to buy cattle at a futures market basis for the month that the cattle are to be slaughtered; and the feeder who accepts the bid determines when to price the cattle. In the case of flat forward contracts, price is set at the time the contract is established.

Grid pricing establishes a baseline price, from which different contract attributes (e.g., quality, yield, grade, and carcass weight) command a specified discount premium. Packers use various techniques for arriving at a base price, including futures prices, boxed beef cutout value, and average price of cattle purchased by the plant in the week prior to the week of slaughter.

Finally, cattle can be sold on the cash market; that is, live cattle are sold at the current market price with no negotiations, contracts, or formulas. Auction sales and sales directly to packers at the spot bid (i.e., cash price) fall into this category.

DEMAND

Worldwide, beef accounts for 20 percent of consumers' meat protein intake and is the third most-consumed meat (excluding fish) on a per capita basis (Economic Research Service/USDA). Global consumption of beef and veal rose 0.4 percent to 49.2 million metric tons in 2004 (*CRB Commodity Yearbook 2005*). The biggest consumers of beef and veal are the United States (12.58 million metric tons/2004), the European Union (8.175 million metric tons/2004), China (6.65 million metric tons), and Brazil (6.41 million metric tons) (*CRB Commodity Yearbook 2005*).

In the United States, beef represented 56 percent of all red meats consumed in 2004 (USDA). Americans consume an average 67 pounds of beef per person per year, including 28 pounds of ground beef, 13 pounds of steaks, and 9 pounds of processed beef (USDA). The highest per capita consumption is in the Midwest (73 pounds), followed by the South and the West (65 pounds each) and the Northeast (63 pounds) (USDA). Low-income consumers tend to eat more beef than do individuals in other-income households (USDA).

The USDA estimated that the United States consumed 27,757 million pounds of beef in 2005, or 65.4 pounds per person. And for 2006, beef consumption is expected to rise only slightly. The USDA forecasts that the United States will consume 27,761 million pounds in 2006, or 65.6 pounds per person.

SUPPLY

World cattle and buffalo figures increased 0.5 percent in 2004 to 1.019 billion head. That total is only a slight advance over the 2003 total of 1.014 billion head, a four-decade low (*CRB Commodity Yearbook 2005*). Global production of beef and veal, on the other hand, climbed 1.2 percent to 50.66 million metric tons in 2004 (*CRB Commodity Yearbook 2005*). The United States is the largest beef producer worldwide, with 11.206 million metric tons of production in 2004, followed by the European Union (8.035 million metric tons), Brazil (7.83 million metric tons), and China (6.683 million metric tons) (*CRB Commodity Yearbook 2005*).

Currently, national cow herds in the United States are in the second year of an expansion phase within a new cattle cycle and numbered a projected 97.102 million head in January 2006 (USDA). Cattle cycles, a series of peaks and troughs in herd size and production, generally last from 8 to 12 years.

United States beef production is expected to climb to 26,052 million pounds in 2006 (USDA/February release), compared with an estimated 24,796 million pounds in 2005. The United States produced 24,650 million pounds of beef in 2004 (USDA).

U.S. beef exports are projected to reach 905 million pounds in 2006, substantially higher than the estimated 669 million pounds exported in 2005 and the 460 million pounds exported in 2004 (USDA). Even so, forecasted 2006 exports represent only 36 percent of the record export level set in 2003 (USDA).

TRADING*

Successful commodity trading requires the ability to estimate the quantity of a commodity at a future point in time based on observations during var-

---

*This section adapted from *CME Livestock Futures and Options: Introduction to Underlying Futures and Options* and *Strategies for CME Livestock Futures and Options* (Chicago Mercantile Exchange Inc., 2005).

ious points in the production cycle. This type of projection, called the pipeline approach to forecasting, views the lifecycle of livestock animals in the food-production process as being in a "pipeline," which the animals enter at birth. It further assumes that, generally speaking, what goes into the pipeline will come out the other end.

Basic requirements for the pipeline approach to forecasting include estimates of current supplies at various points in the pipeline; average time required for a commodity to move from one stage in the pipeline to the next; and information about significant influences on the pipeline flow (e.g., imports, animals diverted from slaughter back into the herd, and significant leakage due to death or exports). The U.S. Department of Agricultural offers much of this information over its web site.

The place to start compiling data for the pipeline approach to forecasting cattle supply is with the size of the cattle crop. The most accurate means of computing the size of a cattle crop is to count cattle placements (in feedlots) or marketings. (Counting newborns is a less reliable method because an unknown number of newborns will die of disease or other causes before achieving market weight.)

The USDA provides monthly estimates of the cattle placed on feed, as well as monthly estimates of cattle already on feed and cattle shipped out of feedlots to slaughter (marketings). Using this information, commodity traders can forecast total commercial slaughter and beef production four to five months in advance.

An inherent weakness in the pipeline approach to forecasting cattle slaughter is that it can be subject to under- or overforecasting, depending on the month in which placements occur. Extremes in weather, for example, can impede the ability of cattle to gain weight properly, thereby delaying their delivery to market and causing slaughter numbers to be lower than anticipated. Insights on weather disruptions as well as other forces that can impact supply (e.g., leakages and infusions) are available in *Livestock, Dairy, and Poultry Situation and Outlook* newsletter, published monthly by the Economic Research Service of the USDA and the *Red Meat Yearbook* data set files.

Commodity traders must also keep in mind *when* cattle imports and exports enter and exit the pipeline. Take, for example, total U.S. slaughter and production numbers, which represent total slaughter and production in the United States. Normally these totals would not be adjusted for exports because most U.S. beef exports are cattle that have been slaughtered in the United States and should therefore be included in total U.S. slaughter and production numbers. U.S. slaughter and production numbers need to be adjusted for exports of *live* animals; however, these animals are slaughtered outside the United States, which removes them from the U.S. production process.

Similarly, only imports of *live* cattle influence U.S. slaughter and production numbers, in that these animals are slaughtered in the United States, which adds them to the U.S. production process. Imports of slaughtered beef, on the other hand, do not impact U.S. production numbers because the animals were not slaughtered in the United States.

To arrive at a forecast of beef production, the trader multiplies the number of head to be slaughtered by the average weight per head (e.g., 745 pounds in 2000). Traders can reduce the margin of error in their estimates by using marketing rather than placements to compute production. Marketing is one stage further along the production pipeline than placements and thus avoids leakage due to death in the feedlot and uncertainties as to how long an animal remains in the feedlot. (Once marketed, the animal goes directly to slaughter.) Counting only marketings also reduces errors due to imports and exports, since cattle are no longer exported from (or imported into) the marketing stage.

CHAPTER 22

Hogs

OVERVIEW

As with cattle, the hog-production cycle begins with the successful birth of pigs into a hog-producing operation. There are three commonly used methods of reproduction. The first entails introducing one or more boars (sexually mature males) into to a herd of sows (mature females that have already reproduced) and gilts (young females that have not reproduced). The second method places a boar together with just one sow or gilt, after which the animals are monitored to ensure that mating takes place. The final method is artificial insemination. It is by far the most labor intensive of the three methods, but it is also the easiest in terms of introducing new genetic content.

Boars are usually purchased by hog producers for reproduction purposes and have a work life of about two years. Sows are bred for two to three years before being sold for slaughter. Mating generally occurs twice a year to ensure a steady flow of new pigs for the production process.

The gestation period for a pig is approximately 110 days, and a sow has an average of 9 to 10 piglets in a litter. The piglets are weaned after three to four weeks, at which point the average litter size has declined to 8.7 piglets due to death from suffocation, disease, weather conditions, or other causes.

Young pigs are separated by sex after weaning in order to more efficiently deal with their differing nutritional requirements. The diet of young pigs is high in grains, generally a mix of corn, barley, milo, and oats. The pigs also receive protein in the form of oilseed mills and vitamin and mineral additives. In the last stages of the feeding process, the pigs generally convert three pounds of feed to one pound of weight, for a gain of about one and a half pounds per day.

Hogs are considered ready for market when they reach about 250 pounds, a process that requires about five months from the time the pig is weaned. The U.S. Department of Agriculture (USDA) reports that the average federally inspected slaughter weight was 262 pounds in 2000, while the carcass weight was 194 pounds.

There are three approaches to the hog-raising process. The first approach—farrow-to-wean operations—raises pigs from birth to three to four weeks, at which time the weaned pigs weigh about 10 to 15 pounds and are sold to a feeding operation. The second—farrow-to-nursery operations—raises pigs from birth to feeder weight (40 to 60 pounds), when the pigs are sent to finishing farms to complete their final weight gain. The last and increasingly popular approach—farrow-to-finish operations—keeps pigs in one place over the entire production process, from birth to slaughter. Pig producers like this vertically integrated approach because it gives them greater control over the quality of their product, that is, over the growth process of their pigs.

In addition to moving toward vertical integration, many hog producers are significantly expanding the size of their operations, which provide economies of scale that improve both feed efficiency and labor productivity. Industry analysts note that production costs decline sharply as marketings increase to 1,000 head and continue to drop, although at a slower rate, as marketings increase over 1,000 head. In 1978, about 67 percent of all marketings came from farms that sold fewer than 1,000 head, whereas in 2000, 78 percent of all marketings came from farms selling over 5,000 head.

The majority of hog-production operations are farrow-to-finish, and most are located in the Western corn belt (68 percent of the nearly 60 million U.S. hog herd/USDA) and the combined areas of Virginia and North Carolina (20 percent of the U.S. hog herd/USDA). New operations are also emerging in Oklahoma and Utah.

Producers sell their market-ready hogs to packers directly or through buying stations and auctions. Most transactions are nonspot transactions; less than a fifth of hog producers sell on the spot market.

Hogs are priced depending on how they are sold. Prices of hogs sold directly are determined relative to the actual percent lean of the hog carcasses (which determines the amount of meat the carcass will yield). Prices of hogs sold at auction, on the other hand, are based on expected percent lean of the hog carcasses.

Hog producers also use marketing contracts to sell their hogs. These contracts can be fixed price, fixed basis, formula basis, cost plus, ledger, price window, and price floor. The following is a quick overview.

- Fixed price agreements, which set an actual price for future delivery, are commonly related to the futures price. They are usually short-term contracts that set the delivery date for one to two months out.
- Fixed basis contracts are similar to fixed price agreements, but rather than setting the actual price, fixed basis contracts set the basis. And because basis agreements apply to a specific futures contract, these fixed basis contracts can last for more than a year.
- Fundamental pricing is derived from a price-determining market. It may entail the addition or subtraction of a price differential due to location or overall quality of the hogs. Fundamental pricing is generally used when a producer forward contracts with a packer or another producer.
- Cost-plus pricing derives from a formula that is generally based on feed costs. It normally sets a minimum price and has a balancing clause.
- Ledger contracts typically last four to seven years and entail making payments to producers when market prices are below a contracted floor price. By the same token, when the contract base price rises above the floor price, producers must pay back money that was received when prices were low.
- Price window agreements are cost-plus agreements with a twist. They generally set a price ceiling and floor between which hogs are exchanged at market price. When prices exceed these limits, however, the buyer and the seller split the difference between the market price and the ceiling or floor price.
- Price floor agreements combine features of ledger and window contracts by setting both a floor price and a ceiling price. A producer places a portion of hog revenues received into a special account whenever hog prices rise above the ceiling price. The producer then draws on the account when prices drop below the floor price.

As with cattle, packers cut hog carcasses into wholesale cuts and ship them to retailers. The yield from a market hog with a live weight of 230 pounds is about 88 pounds of lean meat. Of this amount, 21 percent is ham, 20.3 percent is loin, 13.9 percent is belly (meat used for bacon), 3 percent is spareribs, 7.3 percent is Boston butt roast and blade steaks, and 10.3 percent is picnic (hamlike cut from front leg of hog) (USDA/averages). The remaining 24.2 percent goes to jowl, lean trim, fat, miscellaneous cuts, and trimmings.

DEMAND

World pork consumption rose 2.1 percent to 90.503 million metric tons in 2004 (*CRB Commodity Yearbook 2005*). The USDA estimated world pork consumption increased again in 2005, rising 0.8 percent to 91.197 million metric tons. The United States accounted for 9.9 percent of 2004 worldwide pork consumption, or 8.950 million metric tons (*CRB Commodity Yearbook 2005*), and the USDA estimated that U.S. consumption in 2005 increased by an additional 1 percent to 9.041 million metric tons.

Pork ranks number three in annual U.S. meat consumption behind beef and chicken. Americans consume an average of 51 pounds of pork per capita annually, most of it at home. The Midwest leads in pork consumption (58 pounds per capita) followed by the South (52 pounds), the Northeast (51 pounds), and the West (42 pounds).

Longer term, the Continuing Survey of Food Intakes by Individuals (CSFII) projects declines in per capita consumption of pork in the United States as Hispanics and the elderly—population groups that eat less pork than the national average—become an increasingly bigger share of the overall U.S. population. Total United States pork consumption should continue to expand, however, due to overall growth in the U.S. population (USDA).

SUPPLY

Global pork production rose 2.1 percent in 2004 to 90.858 million metric tons (*CRB Commodity Yearbook 2005*). The USDA estimated an additional 0.8 percent rise in worldwide consumption to 91.619 million metric tons in 2005. Leading world production are China (52 percent of 2004 production), the European Union (23 percent), and the United States (10 percent) (*CRB Commodity Yearbook 2005*).

Global exports of pork climbed 1.6 percent to 4.182 in 2004. The USDA estimated an additional increase in exports of 1.2 percent in 2005 to 4.223 million metric tons. The European Union dominates pork exports with 30 percent of the export total, followed by Canada (23 percent), the United States (22 percent), and Brazil (14 percent) (*CRB Commodity Yearbook 2005*).

The United States is the world's third-largest producer of pork, as well as the largest consumer, exporter, and importer of pork products (USDA). The United States exports about 6 percent of its domestic production, which rose 2.1 percent to 9.332 million metric tons in 2004. U.S. production was estimated to rise an additional 1.9 percent to 95.12 million metric tons in 2005.

The current number of animals in the U.S. hog herd rose 0.1 percent to 60.501 million in 2004 (January 1), its highest level since 1980 (*CRB Commodity Yearbook 2005*). That compares with 466.017 million in China (January 1, 2004) and 152.569 million in Denmark (January 1, 2004), the world's other two largest herds (*CRB Commodity Yearbook 2005*). The total number of hogs worldwide in 2005 is estimated at 810.179 million (January 1) (*CRB Commodity Yearbook 2005*).

TRADING*

To apply the pipeline approach to forecasting hog production, traders need to begin with the size of the pig crop, data that is available from the USDA's National Agricultural Statistics Service (NASS). Additional statistics are also available from the monthly Livestock Slaughter reports, also published by NASS, which provide statistics on total hog slaughter by head; average live and dressed weight in commercial plants by state and in the United States; and information about federally inspected hogs.

Information regarding leakages, infusions, and feedback loops is available from the USDA's Economic Research Service (ERS), which provides data on imports and exports on a monthly basis. The ERS also publishes quarterly and yearly statistics (separated out by selected countries) on a carcass-weight and live-animal basis.

Data on animal retention for purposes of breeding can be found in the *Hogs and Pigs* report (see "Hogs Kept for Breeding" and "Monthly Sows and Gilts Bred") published by the UDSA's NASS. Traders, however, must be aware of variations in data related to whether the industry is in an expansion or a contraction phase.

All of these resources will help traders estimate hog production in a specified time period. For example, by multiplying the number of new pigs born in the United States during the first quarter of 2006 by the average slaughter weight for hogs (250 pounds), traders will approximate the pork production total for the third quarter of 2006 (it takes about two quarters to bring a newborn pig to slaughter weight).

---

*This section adapted from *CME Livestock Futures and Options: Introduction to Underlying Futures and Options* and *Strategies for CME Livestock Futures and Options* (Chicago Mercantile Exchange Inc., 2005).

CHAPTER 23

A Word about Forecasting Supply and Demand in Meats

INTRODUCTION

Forecasts using the pipeline approach provide an estimate of slaughter and production, but they may be inaccurate if investors fail to understand and take into account important forces that impact supply. One of the first things investors need to understand is the *type* of force causing changes in supply. Is change in supply simply due to price fluctuations, or is an external force causing a shift in the entire supply curve?

Theoretically, a supply curve is an upward-sloping line expressing the relationship between the price of a commodity and the quantity supplied. As price increases (decreases), the quantity supplied increases (decreases)—that is, moves either up or down along the existing supply curve. This type of supply change is generally short term and is due solely to changes in the price of a commodity.

Other supply changes are the result of forces that are external to—that is, independent of—the relationship between price and supply. They do not trigger movement up and down the supply curve. Rather, they cause a shift in the supply curve itself. Factors that elicit this type of supply change include changes in the price of inputs, changes in the price of substitutes, changes in the price of joint products, changes in technology, and institu-

This chapter adapted from *CME Livestock Futures and Options: Introduction to Underlying Futures and Options* and *Strategies for CME Livestock Futures and Options* (Chicago Mercantile Exchange Inc., 2005).

tional factors. If the influence of any of these factors is positive, they will cause the supply curve to shift to the right; and if it is negative, the supply curve will shift to the left.

The impact of such factors is long term and may not show up until the next production cycle. This would be the case, for example, if a cattle producer has an incentive to deliver more cattle to market. To do so, the cattle producer would either have to buy more females to increase calf output or buy additional younger animals. In either case, there will be a considerable lapse until new calves are bred and until younger calves have achieved market weight. Only then would the increased supply show up in cattle-production numbers.

Likewise, cattle producers do not cut their herds by eliminating calves already in the production cycle. (They bring those calves to market.) Rather, the producers breed fewer cows going forward, thereby reducing the number of calves in the future. Thus, the impact of the reduction is not evident for some months.

Changes in input prices can have a delayed effect as well. Take, for example, a decline in the price of livestock feed. Cheaper feed should stimulate an increase in the supply of cattle and pigs; but the immediate result is, instead, a drop in the number of livestock. An expansion in supply comes later. That is because at the time of the price drop, it becomes cheaper to achieve each additional pound of weight gain for animals already in the production pipeline. This, in turn, makes it more profitable to feed those animals a little longer than would otherwise be the case, causing a short-term reduction in overall supply.

Supply begins to increase once new animals that have been brought into the pipeline (to profit from the cheaper feed) finally achieve market weight. If all other variables are held constant, decreases in input prices ultimately move the supply curve shift to the right—that is, a larger supply is produced at the same output price. Similarly, increases in input prices (assuming all else remains equal) cause the supply curve to shift to the left— that is, lower quantity is supplied at the same output price.

Changes in the price of substitutes can likewise bring about a shift in the supply curve. Substitutes are alternative products that consumers are willing to purchase to replace a product that is produced with the same resources. Consumers might be willing to replace beef with pork, for example, or vice versa. If the price of product B declines relative to the price of a substitute, such as product A, the supply curve for product A will shift to the right and there will be a greater supply of product A. Likewise, if the price of product B increases relative to product A, the supply curve for product B will shift to the right.

Joint-product prices affect the supply curve by virtue of the close relationship among joint products, which are derived from a single commodity. Pork bellies, spare ribs, and ham, for example, are all joint products (i.e., subproducts) of pork or steer carcasses. Price increases in one of these products, therefore, can shift the supply curve of another joint product to the right, while price decreases can shift the supply curve to the left.

Innovations in the production process of a commodity that result in higher yields without an appreciable change in cost also affect the supply curve. New feed mixtures or additives, for example, can increase the yield of lean meat on a carcass without raising production costs, which would shift the supply curve to the right.

Institutional factors—government programs that affect the commodity-production process by limiting land use or implementing environmental pollution controls—can also have an effect on the supply curve. Guidelines regarding waste disposal at feeder operations, for example, could increase the cost of these operations, making it less profitable to produce livestock, and shift the supply curve to the left.

Substantial interest rate moves—another institutional factor—can also impact supply. Take, for instance, a hike in interest rates that increases financing costs for cattle producers seeking to adopt new technologies or to increase the size of their herds. The higher costs could delay such production improvements. By the same token, a reduction in rates could trigger an escalation of technological innovations, increasing production efficiencies and causing the yield curve to shift to the right (assuming other factors remain constant).

Some factors that result in shifts in the supply curve make their influence felt immediately, rather than over an extended period of time. These include severe weather, disease, and pest outbreaks, which cause the supply curve to shift to the left (assuming all other factors remain constant). In the case of disease, for example, animals will need to be either permanently removed from the supply chain or treated with medications that force their being withheld from the supply chain temporarily. In both instances, the drop in supply of livestock is immediate.

In other cases, factors affecting the supply chain may have both immediate and long-term effects. Under terms of the Dairy Termination Program of 1986, for example, the U.S. government purchased 1.55 million head of cattle from 14,000 dairy farmers and slaughtered the cattle over a period of 18 months. The participating farmers agreed to stay out of the dairy business for at least three years following the sale of their cows to the government. The resulting effect on supply of dairy cattle was therefore both immediate and long-term.

DEMAND

To succeed in commodities investing, investors must also have a good understanding of the factors that influence demand. They must be aware of the close relationship between these factors and consumers' attitudes and purchasing decisions.

As is the case with supply, some factors (i.e., price) trigger movement up and down the demand curve and others cause a shift in the demand curve itself, which is downward sloping. As the price for a commodity rises, demand for the commodity declines—that is, moves lower down the demand curve, resulting in a decreased quantity of the commodity (all else being equal). And when a commodity's price drops, the opposite occurs.

Factors that cause the demand curve itself to shift to the left (negative impact) or the right (positive impact) include a change in the size and distribution of a population, changes in consumer income, changes in the price of substitutes, changes in the price of complements, and changes in consumer preferences.

Let us take a closer look at these factors. There are various ways that a population can change. There can be a demographic shift from a predominantly young to a predominantly aging population. The result would be less demand for children's food and greater need for food appropriate to elderly diets. Or a population may become predominantly urban rather than rural as young people relocate to cities in large numbers to find jobs. Most such changes are long- rather than short-term.

Growth or decline in income levels can also impact demand, although such changes generally affect consumer goods more than food commodities. One food that does reflect changes in income level is meat. Historically, there has been a slight increase in meat consumption when income levels rise, but the biggest impact has been in the cuts of meat consumed. When income rises, demand for more expensive cuts of meat, such as steaks, increases, causing the demand curve for steaks to shift to the right. Similarly, when income declines, demand for expensive cuts of meat declines, causing the demand curve to shift to the left.

Prices of substitutes—goods that can replace other goods—also influence demand for a given commodity. Higher prices for product A, for example, will typically increase demand for a cheaper substitute, product B, and vice versa. In other words, higher prices for product A shift the demand curve for product A to the left, while shifting the demand curve for product B to the right.

Another factor that affects demand is the price of complements, items that enhance a given product but are not required for consumption of the product. Condiments such as ketchup or mustard are good examples of meat complements. Demand for these products generally moves inversely to the price of meat. For example, if the price of pork or beef declines, demand for such condiments typically increases. Similarly, if the price of meat increases, demand for condiments generally declines.

Consumer preferences are the wild card of factors influencing demand. It is very difficult to measure demand-curve shifts that are the result of changes in consumer preference because the changes in preference are themselves not easily isolated or directly observable. They may be the result of advertising, health concerns, or fad diets; and they are often tied to other demand shifters, such as increasing income levels or changing age demographics.

PART SEVEN

Final Considerations

CHAPTER 24

Commodity Funds

Public commodity funds evolved from the idea of mutual funds. That is to say, investors would entrust their capital to professional managers who, in return for a fee and a percentage of the profits, would make investments with the purpose of increasing the capital at their disposal. The more common form is organized as a limited partnership. The speculator invests around $5,000 in "units" of the partnership, which are redeemable at net asset value by the partnership. Unlike a position in futures contracts, the speculator can only lose his or her $5,000 investment.

There are some risk factors:

- *Commodity futures trading is speculative.* Commodity futures prices are highly volatile. Price movements of commodity futures contracts are influenced by changing supply-and-demand relationships; by weather; by government, agricultural, trade, fiscal, and monetary and exchange control programs and policies; by national and international political and economic events; and by changes in interest rates. In addition, governments from time to time do intervene, directly and by regulation, in certain markets, particularly in currencies and gold. Such intervention is often intended to directly influence prices.

- *Commodity futures trading may be illiquid.* Most United States commodity exchanges limit the fluctuations in commodity futures contract prices during a single day by regulations referred to as the "daily price fluctuation limit" or "daily limit." During a single trading day, no trades may be executed at prices beyond the daily limit. Once the price of a futures contract has reached the daily limit for that day, positions in that contract can be neither taken nor liquidated. Commodity futures prices have occasionally moved the daily limit for several consecutive days with little or no trading. Similar occurrences could prevent the partnership from promptly liquidating unfavorable positions and could subject the partnership to substantial losses that could exceed the margin initially committed to such trades. In addition, even if commodity futures prices have not moved the daily limit, the partnership may not be able to execute future trades at favorable prices if little trading in such contracts is taking place. Any governmental imposition of price controls may also inhibit price movements in the commodity markets, to the significant detriment of the partnership.

- *Commodity futures trading is highly leveraged.* The low-margin deposits normally required in commodity futures trading permit an extremely high degree of leverage. Accordingly, a relatively small price movement in a commodity futures contract may result in immediate and substantial loss to the investor. For example, if at the time of purchase, 10 percent of the price of the futures contract is deposited as margin, a 10 percent decrease in the price of the futures contract would, if the contract were then closed out, result in a total loss of the margin deposit before any deduction for the trading commission. Thus, like other leveraged investments, any futures trade may result in losses in excess of the amount invested. Although the partnership may lose more than its initial margin in a trade, the partnership, and not the limited partners personally, will be subject to margin calls. The partnership is also subject to the risk of failure of any of the exchanges in which it trades.

- *Commodity futures trading is subject to speculative position limits.* The Commodities Futures Trading Commission (CFTC) and certain exchanges have established limits referred to as "speculative position limits" or "position limits" on the maximum net-long or net-short futures position that any person may hold or control in particular commodities. The CFTC has jurisdiction to establish position limits with respect to all commodities traded in exchanges located in the United States, and any exchange may then impose additional limits on positions on that exchange. These modifications of trades of the partnerships, if required, could adversely affect the operations and profitability of the partnerships.

- *A variation on the above is the commodity hedge fund marketed to high net-worth investors.* The minimum investment usually starts at $250,000, which the investor commits for a minimum term of three years. The investor is usually provided with an annual update on the fund's return, but is provided no information on the commodities traded.

CHAPTER 25

Sources of Market Information

A good speculator needs to have timely market information at his or her disposal at all times. This chapter describes the reports that are available.

GRAINS

Corn, Wheat, Oats, and the Soybean Complex of Soybeans, Soybean Meal, and Soybean Oil

The U.S. Department of Agriculture (USDA) issues monthly crop production reports through its Crop Reporting Board (CRB). These reports provide information for various field crops, including prospective plantings, planted acreage yields, and production.

The Agricultural Statistics Board (www.nass.usda.gov) publishes free reports. Write to USDA, Washington, DC 20250.

Expected Plantings.   In the spring, the USDA releases various field crop reports (www.nass.usda.gov). These reports cover all of the major grains. A prospective plantings report is also released then. The report contains expected plantings as of the first of the month for corn, oats, and other spring wheat.

In December, the small grains report indicates acreage, yield, and production of wheat and oats, plus revised data for the previous year.

Quarterly grain stocks reports generally include stocks of all wheat, corn, oats, and soybeans by state. These are released in January, April, June, and October. Because the October release excludes soybean stocks, a separate soybean stocks report is issued in September.

The USDA publishes a weekly grain market news report containing data about grains inspected for export, barge loading, and prices.

Grain Utilization.   Five times yearly, the feed situation reports give updates about grain utilization and government price support program activities.

For wheat traders, a wheat situation report is published four times yearly. It summarizes wheat fundamentals and gives information about world developments, current outlook, government programs, and prospects for the coming year.

The fats and oils situation reports, issued five times yearly, offer professional comment on general economic conditions affecting soybeans and soybean oil. These reports also show yield, disappearance, crushings, and exports.

Monthly agricultural prices reports show prices received by farmers for principal crops. Special articles may also appear.

The annual agricultural prices report in June provides a summary of indexes of prices farmers received and paid the previous year. A crop value report in January offers season average prices and value of production for principal crops.

The USDA offers a *Weekly Weather and Crop Bulletin* (usda.mannlib .cornell.edu/reports/nassr/field/weather/) summarizing weather and its effect on crops for the previous week.

For almost all commodities, traders might find helpful the monthly *Commitment of Traders in Commodity Futures* report from the Commodity Futures Trading Commission (CFTC). This report gives the open interest of holders of long and short positions in a detailed breakout, according to position type and size.

The Chicago Board of Trade, 141 W. Jackson Blvd., Chicago, IL 60604, also is a valuable information source for grains. Besides various brochures for each contract, the exchange publishes a statistical annual, listing historical spot and futures prices plus a plethora of other useful data. Contact the Chicago Board of Trade's literature services. It also offers a free weekly statistical summary through its market information department.

MEATS

Live Cattle, Feeder Cattle, Live Hogs, Frozen Pork Bellies, and Iced Broiler Chickens

In January and July, the USDA releases its cattle inventory numbers. These two reports include the number and value of all cattle and calves as of the first of the month by states. Monthly cattle-on-feed reports reveal the total number of cattle on feed, placements, marketings, and other disappearance for seven selected states. Special 23-state cattle-on-feed reports issued four times yearly give for 23 states the information just mentioned and add expected marketings.

The USDA releases four hogs and pigs reports each year. The March, June, September, and December reports show inventory figures and hog numbers by classes. Also included are expected farrowings and pig-crop data for selected periods. The December report adds the number of hog operations by state and inventory by size groups for major producing states.

Monthly livestock slaughter reports give the number of head and live weights of cattle, calves, hogs, sheep, and lambs slaughtered, plus red meat production by species and lard production for the nation.

In March, the annual summary details total livestock slaughter and red meat and lard production for the previous year by states.

In April, the USDA publishes its *Meat Animals: Production, Disposition, and Income* for the previous year (usda.mannlib.cornell.edu/reports/nassr/livestock/zma-bb/). For poultry, a weekly broiler hatchery report shows the number of broiler chicks placed and broiler-type eggs set for the previous week in 21 states.

A monthly eggs, chickens, and turkeys report designates the number of layers on hand, the number of eggs per 100 layers, and other data. Special monthly reports offer additional information, such as the number and value of chickens on hand.

Monthly poultry slaughter reports reveal the number of head and pounds slaughtered under federal inspection.

In April, the USDA issues *Broiler Hatchery*, *Chickens and Eggs*, and *Turkey Hatchery*—as well as annual reports on hatchery production and layers and egg production, which are offered in March and January, respectively.

For all meats, monthly cold storage reports give figures for holdings of meats and poultry products for the end of the previous month. Regional cold storage holdings reports come out in March.

The USDA's Agricultural Marketing Service (AMS) compiles *Livestock*

Market News every week and *Poultry Market News* three times a week. Each report contains cash market information, such as slaughter estimates, prices, and supply-demand narratives.

For hogs and pork bellies, the hog-corn ratio is available from many nongovernmental sources. Other statistics are available in *The National Provisioner Magazine* (http://www.nationalprovisioner.com/mediakit.php).

The Chicago Mercantile Exchange, 444 W. Jackson Blvd., Chicago, IL 60606, lists the meat complex contracts. It offers daily information bulletins. These relate both the futures and the cash prices plus other information such as USDA slaughter figures and cold storage movement. A statistical yearbook that shows past futures and cash prices may also be purchased. Contact the Chicago Mercantile Exchange's office services division for both publications.

Also relevant to the cattle trade are the USDA's pasture and range conditions reports, released nine times a year as part of the crop-production reports.

FOODS

Sugar, Coffee, Cocoa, Orange Juice, and Potatoes

Weather and international factors such as political tensions, currency stability, income level, and trade policies are especially influential for sugar, coffee, cocoa, and orange juice. Obtaining accurate estimates of foreign coffee, cocoa, and orange juice production is particularly difficult. The USDA releases periodic crop-production and crop-value estimates for all the food commodities.

A monthly sugar market statistics report lists sugar distribution, prices, stocks, and supply. A weekly sugar distribution report is also available from the USDA.

For sugar and coffee, a branch of the USDA publishes foreign agricultural circulars that relay statistics and general comments about world production and stocks.

The Census Bureau, Washington, DC 20233, issues a report on coffee, *Green Coffee: Inventories, Imports, and Roastings.*

Reports on weekly main-crop purchases by the market boards of Ghana, West Africa, and Nigeria start in October and reflect the major supply of cocoa available for export.

In October, the USDA gives a series of world cocoa production estimates. The Census Bureau also offers a monthly report on United States confectionery stores, which covers the poundage and dollar sales of chocolate items.

LIST COMMODITIES

The weekly USDA crop production estimates for orange juice begin in October. Weekly movement figures indicate consumption and orange juice imports. A crops values report comes out in January, and a citrus fruits report is offered by the USDA in September.

Monthly cold storage reports from the USDA indicate frozen orange juice stocks. The Florida Department of Citrus makes its own periodic estimates of Florida's and Brazil's crops.

The USDA's July, September, October, and January crop-production reports include information about potatoes. A potatoes and sweet potatoes report in September offers comprehensive data about potato acreage, disposition, and also utilization, value, production, prices, and monthly marketings.

The USDA's Agricultural Marketing Service issues weekly cotton market news, while the CRB offers prospective plantings reports in the spring and acreage figures in early summer. Crop-production reports come out about eight times a year. A crop-value report is offered in January.

The Census Bureau releases specific reports about the use of cotton in products and the amount of cotton ginned. Three reports offered include the monthly *Cotton Manmade Fiber Staple & Linters* (consumption stocks and spindle activity), *General Imports of Cotton Manufacturers*, and *Woven Fabrics: Production and Unfilled Orders*.

Stumpage costs, an indicator of available lumber supplies, represent costs of buying standing timber from government land or maintaining co-owned forests. These figures and others are available from the Western Wood Products Association (www.wwpa.org). Other information includes figures on production, orders, shipments, weekly inventories, inland mill sales, and past price summaries. For a free list of publications, request the *Subscription Rates for Statistical Reports* from the association's statistical department.

The USDA's Forest Service gives information about general trends in timber supply and demand.

Lastly, the Federal Reserve reports on general economic conditions important to construction.

Glossary of Common Commodity Trading Terms

Accumulate   When traders buy a commodity heavily and "take it out of the market."

Actuals   Commodities on hand, ready for shipment, storage, or manufacture.

Afloats   Commodities loaded on vessels and on way to destination. It may refer to loaded boats in harbor and about to sail, but not to cargoes already at destination.

Arbitrage   Simultaneous purchase and sale of the same quantity of the same commodity in two different markets, either in the same country or in different countries. Used to take advantage of what is believed to be a temporary disparity in prices.

At the market   An order to buy or sell at the best price obtainable at the time the order reached the trading pit or ring.

Basis   The price difference over or under a designated future at which a commodity of a certain description is sold or quoted.

Basis grade   Specified grade, or grades, named in the exchange's futures contract. Other grades are tenderable, subject to price differentials from the basis, or "contract" grade.

Bid   A bid subject to immediate acceptance, made on the floor of an exchange to buy a definite quantity of a commodity future at a specified price; opposite of *offer*. See also *Offer*.

Break   A quick, extensive decline in prices.

Bulge   A rapid advance in prices.

Buy on close   To buy at the end of a trading session at a price within the closing range.

Buy on opening   To buy at the beginning of a trading session at a price within the opening range.

C&F (cost and freight)   Cost and freight paid to port of destination.

Carrying charge Usually refers to warehouse charges, insurance, and other incidentals, often including interest charge and estimated loss (or gain) in weight. When used in connection with delivery against futures, this term includes weighing, sampling, taring, checking of weights, repairing, repiling, labor to scales, and so on.

Cash commodity The actual physical product, as distinguished from the "future." See also *Spot commodity*.

CCC Commodity Credit Corporation.

Certified stocks or certified supplies Supplies that have been approved as deliverable grades and often graded as to quality. Such gradings hold good for a specified period or for an indefinite time. Some exchanges list established deterioration schedules.

CFTC Commodities Futures Trading Commission.

CIF Cost, insurance, and freight paid or included to port of destination.

Clearances Total marine shipments of a specified commodity as of a given date from domestic and foreign ports.

Close The period at the end of the trading session officially designated by the exchange during which all transactions are considered made "at the close."

Closing price or range The price or price range recorded during the period designated by the exchange as the official close.

Commission house A concern that buys and sells actual commodities or futures contracts for the accounts of customers.

Contract grades Those grades of a commodity that have been officially approved by an exchange as deliverable in settlement of a futures contract.

Cover The cancellation of a short position in any future by the purchase of an equal quantity of the same future. See also *Liquidation*.

Crop year Period from the harvest of a crop to the corresponding period in the following year, as used statistically. U.S. wheat crop year begins June 1 and ends May 31; cotton, August 1 to July 31; varying dates for other commodities.

Day orders Orders at a limited price are understood to be good for the day only, unless expressly designated as an open order or good till canceled order.

Deliverable grades See *Contract grades*.

Delivery The tender and receipt of the actual commodity, or warehouse receipts covering such commodity, in settlement of a futures contract.

Delivery month A specified month within which delivery may be made under the terms of a futures contract.

Delivery notice A notice of a clearing member's intention to deliver a stated quantity of a commodity in settlement of a futures contract.

Delivery points   Those points designated by futures exchanges at which the physical commodity covered by a futures contract may be delivered in fulfillment of such contract.

Differentials   The premiums paid for the grades better than the basis grade, and the discounts allowed for the grades lower than the basis grades. These differentials are fixed by the contract terms on most exchanges; but in cotton, commercial differentials or differences apply.

Evening up   When for any reason traders are completing their transactions by selling in the case of longs or by purchasing in the case of shorts, they are said to be "evening up."

EX-store   Selling term for commodities in warehouse.

FAQ   Fair average quality.

Farm prices   The prices received by farmers for their products, as published by the U.S. Department of Agriculture, as of the 15th of each month.

First notice day   First day on which transferable notices can be issued for delivery in specified delivery month.

FOB   Free on board. Usually covers cost of putting commodities on board whatever shipment conveyance is being used.

Forward shipment   This type of contract covers actual commodities to be shipped at some future specified date.

Futures   A term used to designate any or all contracts covering the sale of commodities for future delivery made on an exchange and subject to its rules.

Grades   Various qualities according to accepted trade usage.

Grading certificates   Certificates attesting to quality of a commodity graded by official inspectors, testers, graders, and so on.

Growths   Description of commodity according to area of growth; refers to country, district, or place of semimanufacture.

GTC   Good till canceled. Usually refers to open orders to buy or sell at a fixed price.

Hedge   A sale of any commodity for further delivery on or subject to the rules of any futures market to the extent that such sales are offset in quantity by the ownership or purchase of the same cash commodity; or, conversely, purchases of any commodity for future delivery on or subject to the rules of any futures market to the extent that such purchases are offset by sales of the same cash commodity.

Invisible supply   Usually refers to uncounted stocks in hands of wholesalers, manufacturers, and ultimate consumers; sometimes to producers' stocks that cannot be accurately counted.

Life of delivery   Period between first and last trade in any futures delivery contract.

Limited order   An order given to a broker by a customer that has some restrictions upon its execution, such as price or time.

Liquidation   A transaction made in reducing or closing out a long or short position, but more often used by the trade to mean a reduction or closing out of a long position. See also *Cover*.

Loan prices   The prices at which producers may obtain loans from the government for their crops.

Long   (1) The buying side of an open futures contract. (2) A trader whose net position in the futures market shows an excess of open purchases over open sales.

Lot   Usually any definite quantity of a commodity of uniform grade; the standard unit of trading in the futures market.

Margin   Cash or equivalent posted as guarantee of fulfillment of a futures contract (not a part payment or purchase). Can be designated as *original* or *variation margin*.

Margin call   Demand for additional funds, or equivalent, because of adverse price movement or some other contingency.

Market order   An order for immediate execution at the best available price.

Negotiable warehouse receipt   Document issued by warehouse, which guarantees existence and often specifies grade of commodity stored. Facilitates transfer of ownership by endorsement of receipt's owner.

Net position   The difference between the open contracts long and the open contracts short held in any one commodity by any individual or group.

Nominal price or nominal quotation   Price quotations on a future and for a period in which no actual trading took place.

Offer   The willingness to sell at a given price; the opposite of *bid*. See also *Bid*.

On opening   A term used to specify execution of an order during the opening.

Open contracts   Contracts that have been bought or sold without the transaction having been completed by subsequent sale, or repurchase, or actual delivery or receipt of commodity.

Open interest   The number of "open contracts." It refers to unliquidated purchases or sales and never to their combined total.

Open order   An order that is good until canceled.

Opening, The   The period at the beginning of the trading session officially designated by the exchange during which all transactions are considered made "at the opening."

Opening price or range   The price or price range recorded during the period designated by the exchange as the official opening.

Pit   An octagonal platform on the trading floor of an exchange, consisting of steps upon which traders and brokers stand while executing futures trades. See also *Ring*.

Point   The minimum unit in which changes in futures price may be expressed. (Minimum price fluctuation may be in multiples of points.)

Position   An interest in the market in the form of open commitments.

Premium   The amount by which a given future or quality of a spot commodity sells over another future or quality of a spot commodity.

Price limit   The maximum fluctuation in price of a futures contract permitted during one trading session, as fixed by the rules of a contract market.

Primary markets   When used in connection with foreign-produced commodities, refers to country of production. In domestic commodities, refers to centers that receive commodities directly from country shippers.

Purchase and sale statement (P&S)   A statement sent by a commission merchant to a customer when his or her futures position has been reduced to closed out. It shows the amount involved; the price at which the position was acquired and reduced or closed out, respectively; the gross profits or loss; the commission charged; and the net profit or loss on the transaction.

Range   The difference between the high and the low price of the future during a given period.

Reaction   The downward tendency of a commodity after an advance.

Realizing   When a profit is realized either by a liquidating sale or the repurchase of a short sale.

Resting order   Instruction to buy or sell at figures away from the current level.

Ring   A circular platform on the trading floor of an exchange, consisting of steps upon which traders and brokers stand while executing futures trades. See also *Pit*.

Round lot   The trading unit in which the major portion of trading occurs on those exchanges that make provisions for trading in two different units; prices of transactions in such units only are registered as official quotations.

Round turn   The execution for the same principal of a purchase transaction and a sales transaction that offset each other.

Short   (1) The selling of an open futures contract. (2) A trader whose net position in the futures market shows all excess of open sales over open purchases. See also *Long*.

Spot commodity   The actual physical commodity, as distinguished from the futures. See also *Cash commodity*.

Spot price   The price at which the spot or cash commodity is selling. In grain trading, it is called the "cash" price.

Stop loss order or stop   An order that only takes place when the market reaches the level mentioned in the order. Its purpose is to limit losses. It may be either a buying order or a selling order An example would be "Sell Two October Cotton at 37.50 Stop." This indicates the person has bought at a price higher than 37.50 and wants to limit his or her loss to around the 37.50 level.

Straddle   Usually refers to purchase in one market and simultaneous sale of same commodity in some other market. It can refer to purchase of one commodity against sale of a different commodity, both of which should normally be closely allied in price movements.

Switching   Simultaneously buying a contract for futures delivery in one month while selling a contract of the same commodity in another delivery month on the same exchange.

Tenders   Issuance of transferable notices announcing intention of tendering or delivering actual commodity.

Transferable notice   Notice given by the seller of a futures contract that he or she has made preparation for actual delivery.

Visible supply   Usually refers to supplies of a commodity in recognized distribution centers, which have been moved from production areas to shipping centers. It varies with different commodities and often includes afloats and all other supplies "in sight."

Volume of trading or sales   Represents a simple addition of successive futures transactions. (A transaction consists of a purchase and a matching sale.)

Wire house   A firm operating a private wire to its own branch offices or to other firms.

Index